THE COUNTING H

*"A true Christian, as well as a man
of great acuteness and tried integrity"*

A description of Thomas Thompson
by William Wilberforce, in a letter
to Arthur Young, August 1797.

The Counting House

Thomas Thompson of Hull (1754-1828) and his family

by

Arthur R.B. Robinson

William Sessions Limited
York, England

ISBN 1 85072 102 5

Printed by
William Sessions Limited
The Ebor Press, York, England

Contents

List of Illustrations

Preface and Acknowledgements

Soon after Thomas Thompson's death in 1828, Mr Charles Frost told the Hull Literary & Philosophical Society that "Mr Thompson was so intimately known to many, and so highly respected by all, as to render any formal eulogy of his talents and virtues unnecessary"[51].

One hundred and sixty four years later, that is no longer the case. Thomas Thompson's name is known to descendants, and among East Yorkshire historians, and his portrait hangs in the Hull Docks Museum; but even in Hull he is sometimes confused with his son Thomas Perronet Thompson, or with another Thomas Thompson, sometime Mayor of Hull, whose bust is in the Guildhall. More importantly, perhaps, his life is overshadowed by that of his friend and contemporary William Wilberforce, who had less to do with Hull than did Thompson, but who will always be better remembered there.

Thompson deserves to be "intimately known" once again. Born in a small village, this man began a banking and business career which he pursued successfully and honestly, through times of peace and war, for over half a century. He underwent an experience of Christian conversion which influenced his life, in very positive ways, for sixty years. He and his wife, whose family had worked closely with the Wesleys, brought up four talented children, each successful in a different way. Thompson himself spent twelve years in Parliament, during and after the Napoleonic Wars, believing that Providence had placed him there to promote good causes, and acting on that belief. He achieved a great deal both for the commerce and for the poor of Hull and Cottingham. Finally, he kept a journal, full of detailed observation and comment on national, local and family events of the years 1814 to 1827.

His wife, too, wrote fluently, and we learn much about her character, and the characters of her children, from letters which she wrote and which have survived. This book is, therefore, a *family* biography of a man, his wife, and their children, in a particularly interesting period of history. To set bounds on the book, I have kept it to the years of Thompson's own life, 1754 to 1828.

Six years ago, I simply knew that Thomas Thompson and his wife were among my thirty-two great great great grandparents. They had a very modest place in family papers which I had inherited, many of them assembled by Edith Thompson[4], a historian and great grand-daughter of Thomas Thompson.

(51) This, and similar references throughout the text, are to the same number in the Bibliography.

In 1985, however, my wife and I moved to York. We made our first contact with Hull and Holderness, where friendly local historians knew something of Thomas Thompson, and shared that knowledge. I then found that Johnson's biography of Thomas Perronet Thompson[6] put flesh on Thomas Thompson's bones. Hansard's records of Thompson's speeches in Parliament showed more of his versatility. Next, his wife's letters[2], preserved by my cousin Jessica Thompson, brought Mrs Thompson and her children into sharper focus. Leighton-Boyce's book[7] set out Thompson's considerable talents as a banker. Then, unexpectedly, I came across an early account of him as a preacher. Finally I discovered, with great delight, that another cousin, Martin Thompson, had Thompson's complete journals. Until then, I had only known extracts from them.

This book draws all those strands together for the first time. Johnson used Edith Thompson's many papers — then in family hands, but now distributed between the Brynmor Jones Library, Hull, and the Brotherton Library, Leeds — for his comprehensive life of Thomas Perronet Thompson, published in 1957[6]. In 1958 he gave an excellent account of Thomas Thompson's own life in a lecture to the Cottingham Local History Society[32]. That lecture indicated that he had read Leighton-Boyce's book, then recently published, and had perused Thompson's journals. My own use of those journals, however, goes much further; and I have been able to give very much more detail about Thompson and his family from a wide range of sources.

The bibliography shows the number of early nineteenth century records which I have drawn upon. This has involved the cooperation of librarians, keepers of local records and clergy in a number of parts of the country, and I greatly appreciate their help. In Hull and East Yorkshire I readily acknowledge specific help from the following, alphabetically: Geoffrey Bell, Arthur Credland, Ann Emery, Eileen & Kenneth Green, Robert Holtby and John Markham. Oliver Beckerlegge gave particular help in York. Martin Thompson lent me Thompson's journals, as mentioned above. Jessica Thompson gave me the wisdom of her own researches, along with Mrs Thompson's letters. Nigel Hughes lent me Mrs Thompson's journal of a tour of Scotland. Fay Dixon typed many pages for me. Bob Sissons of Ebor Press gave much advice on their production. At the end of it all, this book would not have been printed without the financial assistance of several descendants of Thomas Thompson and his wife. I thank them, and particularly Benedict & Catherine Thompson-McCausland, who coordinated that help.

Finally I thank my wife Betty, who has lived with this book for a long time, for all her encouragement of my researches, and for all her help with their presentation.

York, 1992.

Notes on the names 'Perronet', 'Philothea' and 'Thompson' in the text

DAVID PERRONET OF CHATEAU D'OEX near Lake Geneva came to England in 1681 and married Philothea Arthur. Their son was Vincent Perronet, shown in an illustration and in the genealogical table. The same table shows that Perronet became used as a Christian name. It is still so used down to the present generation.

The name Philothea has also continued to the present time. The second syllable is accented, and pronounced 'oh'. Although often believed to be the feminine version of Theophilus of the New Testament, 'beloved of God', it is not an exact equivalent.

I am aware that it may not always be easy for the reader to distinguish Thomas Thompson (1754-1828) from his son Thomas Perronet Thompson. Johnson, in his biography of the son, always called him 'Perronet', perhaps because he signed his name 'T. Perronet Thompson'; but I myself have found no document in which his parents, brothers or sister called him anything but 'Thomas'. In this book I have generally called the father 'Thomas Thompson', or simply 'Thompson'; and have either called Thomas Perronet Thompson 'his son Thomas', or have given his full name.

A similar difficulty may sometimes confuse Philothea Perronet Thompson the mother with Philothea Thompson the daughter. I have generally called the mother 'Mrs Thompson' (feeling that she would not resent that formality), and have reserved 'Philothea' for her daughter.

Map of Holderness, 1822. Engraved by Consitt & Goodwill for Thomas Thompson's History of Holderness *(1824).*

CHAPTER 1

Holderness, Hull and Hoxton
1753-1781

THOMAS THOMPSON WAS BORN IN 1754 in Holderness, the part of East Yorkshire which lies between the Wolds and the sea.

Today, a main road carries you quickly from Hull, at the southern edge of Holderness, to Bridlington at its northern tip. Between Coniston and Skirlaugh, a farm called Owbrough, formerly Owbrough Grange, stands on the right of the road. It is Thomas Thompson's birthplace. Turnings to the left are signposted to Swine.

Mid-eighteenth century maps show lanes winding much more vaguely and muddily through the village of Swine, past Owbrough Grange, and on through Holderness. When Thompson wrote, in later life, ''I was born in the parish of Swine, at Woldbrough or Owbrough Grange, which was formerly a Farm or Grange belonging to the Cistercian nuns at Swine''[1][*], he was describing an area which was very rural and isolated, despite its proximity to the port of Hull.

His parents, Francis Thompson and Ann Torrington, were villagers who had married at Swine church in 1750. Three of their children besides Thomas survived to adulthood. William, born in 1751, became an attorney. Anne, born in 1764 and named after an older sister who had died, married an attorney. Jane, born in 1767[66], did not marry, and gave considerable help to her brother Thomas and his children. There is a memorial tablet to Anne and Jane in Beverley Minster.

Thomas Thompson's first schooling was under the Rev William Stead, Vicar of Swine. ''The Vicars of Swine within the last century have not been remarkable either for their learning or their piety'', he recalled; and he seemed to include Mr Stead in that category. Fortunately his parents had ambitions for him, and he went on to a school at Brandesburton, eight miles away, ''for the purpose of being better prepared for the business of a merchant's counting house, either in England or abroad''[1]. It seems likely that this was the school set up by the Mason and Barker charity, where — at any rate when Poulson described it in 1840 — seventeen poor children were taught free, and others could pay to attend. Boys were taught reading, writing and accounts. Girls were taught reading, knitting and sewing, ''and writing if their parents wish it''[56]. Thompson's school life was not easy, it seems. He suffered ''various hardships there which I well remember'', but which he does not specify.

Looking back at the age of sixty, he remembered his father's mother. Born Mary Pinder, she was probably a daughter of William Pinder, Hull master mariner[91]. ''She was a woman of considerable talents'', wrote her grandson, ''and was skilled in accounts far above most other women in Holderness. Through her prudence and industry, various purchases of land were made for the benefit of her husband and children''[1]. Her son Francis Thompson — Thomas' father — farmed land at Catwick which amounted to 'seven sheep gates yearly, upon such cornfields as happen to lie fallow, and a beast

1

*) Throughout this book, a number in brackets above the text refers to the same numbered source in the Bibliography.

gate in the average [sic] field of Catwick'[56]. He also had a long lease of a farm in Swine[1], which was presumably Owbrough Grange.

Thomas Thompson remembered that his father had a great respect for learning, but also that he "lacked judgment and sobriety of conduct"[1]. Rural life was a hard, monotonous grind. Holderness, at that time, was isolated and continuously subject to winter flooding[1]. John Wesley, as he travelled the country, wrote in 1766 that "In general the life of English country farmers is supremely dull. ... Of all the people in the kingdom, they are the most discontented, seldom satisfied either with God or man"[90]. Those may have been the sentiments of Francis Thompson. At any rate, one source says that he was, "like many farmers in those days, engaged in doing a little 'fair trade', or smuggling. He was taken prisoner, and ended his days in a Dutch prison"[5]. Another source says that "smuggling did not put him on his feet, and when, during a war, he turned privateer, ill-luck still pursued him, and he died a prisoner of the French"[37].

Jack Dykes describes the extent of smuggling along the whole length of the Yorkshire coast at that time. Spirits, tobacco, quicksilver, tea and a variety of other goods were regularly brought in from France and Holland, sometimes in exchange for Yorkshire wool, which it was illegal to export. In Holderness alone, small detachments of Scots Greys, Inniskillings or other dragoons would be based at Hedon, Patrington, Aldbrough, Hornsea, Skipsea and Bridlington Quay to assist the Customs and Excise men, but they did not prevent the trade going on[24]. Thomas Thompson says nothing about his father's part in it, except that "the maintenance of an affectionate mother and of two Sisters devolved upon me"; that he himself placed his sisters in such schools as he could afford[1]; that his mother died in 1777[66], "worn down by various afflictions"[1]; and that his father "lived several years afterwards, and after various irregularities of which it is not necessary to speak, died in France"[1].

"A defect in the Will of a relative" seems to have deprived young Thompson of one more source of money to help him in a business career[1]. He therefore stood very much on his own feet when in 1770, as a youth of sixteen, he entered the counting house of William Wilberforce, Russia and Baltic merchant[7]. This Wilberforce was grandfather of the slave emancipator, or, as Thompson put it, "grandfather of the Member for Yorkshire"[1]. The old merchant, said Thompson, was "a man of the first character in Hull. His talent and education were superior to those of many of his neighbours"[1]. However, he was then eighty years old and living at North Ferriby[54]. His son Robert had succeeded him in the business, but had himself died in 1768. Robert Wilberforce's place had been taken by his nephew Abel Smith II[7] (1748-1779)[54], son of the banker Abel Smith of Nottingham and brother of Robert Smith, later Lord Carrington [see genealogical table]. Thus the firm of Wilberforce had become Wilberforce & Smith when Thomas Thompson joined it in 1770. It operated from 25 High Street, now the Wilberforce Museum[7], which stood with its front to the busy street and its back to the bustling staithes on the River Hull.

Anxious to improve himself, young Thompson used his hours of "relaxation from business" to study Greek, Latin and French, assisted by a Mr Little, a Hull schoolmaster confined in the prison which stood at the south end of the market place until 1792[19]. "Mr Little was a very convenient associate", Thompson observed, "because he was always stationary. Thus, all my time was filled up from an early hour in the morning to a late hour at night, and by the mercy of God I was preserved from those vices into which young men in populous towns are in continuous danger of falling"[1].

Meanwhile, two hundred miles away, Thomas Thompson's future wife was growing up. Her name was Philothea Perronet Briggs[*] and her parents lived at Hoxton Square, Shoreditch, on the north side of the City of London. Her father, William Briggs, was son of a Rector of Holt in Norfolk, and grandson of William Briggs, physician to William III. He himself was an

(*) See Preface for origin and pronunciation of the name Philothea.

Members of the Thompson family, and other relatives, mentioned in the text

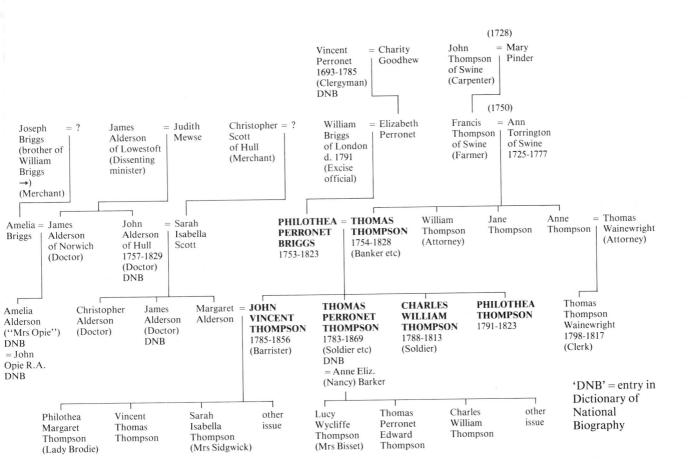

Vincent Perronet 1693-1785 (Clergyman) DNB = Charity Goodhew

(1728) John Thompson of Swine (Carpenter) = Mary Pinder

Joseph Briggs (brother of William Briggs →) (Merchant) = ?

James Alderson of Lowestoft (Dissenting minister) = Judith Mewse

Christopher Scott of Hull (Merchant) = ?

William Briggs of London d. 1791 (Excise official) = Elizabeth Perronet

(1750) Francis Thompson of Swine (Farmer) = Ann Torrington of Swine 1725-1777

Amelia Briggs = James Alderson of Norwich (Doctor)

John Alderson of Hull 1757-1829 (Doctor) DNB = Sarah Isabella Scott

PHILOTHEA PERRONET BRIGGS 1753-1823 = **THOMAS THOMPSON** 1754-1828 (Banker etc)

William Thompson (Attorney)

Jane Thompson

Anne Thompson = Thomas Wainewright (Attorney)

Amelia Alderson ("Mrs Opie") DNB = John Opie R.A. DNB

Christopher Alderson (Doctor)

James Alderson (Doctor) DNB

Margaret Alderson = **JOHN VINCENT THOMPSON** 1785-1856 (Barrister)

THOMAS PERRONET THOMPSON 1783-1869 (Soldier etc) DNB = Anne Eliz. (Nancy) Barker

CHARLES WILLIAM THOMPSON 1788-1813 (Soldier)

PHILOTHEA THOMPSON 1791-1823

Thomas Thompson Wainewright 1798-1817 (Clerk)

Philothea Margaret Thompson (Lady Brodie)

Vincent Thomas Thompson

Sarah Isabella Thompson (Mrs Sidgwick)

other issue

Lucy Wycliffe Thompson (Mrs Bisset)

Thomas Perronet Edward Thompson

Charles William Thompson

other issue

'DNB' = entry in Dictionary of National Biography

3

excise official, who combined that profession with zealous work for the Methodist cause. He led one of the 'bands' — groups of inner members — at the Foundery[22], Wesley's meeting place in the City Road, not far from Hoxton. Members of 'bands' examined one another's spiritual progress, and William Briggs had not been afraid to advise John Wesley himself, in 1750. "I think you feel not, abidingly, a deep sense of your own spiritual weakness, the nearness of Christ to save, nor a sweet communion with the Holy Spirit", wrote Briggs to Wesley. "You have the appearance of all Christian graces; but they do not, I think, spring from a deep experience"[82]. Wesley may have appreciated Briggs' frankness. At any rate, he made Briggs one of his first two Book Stewards, with responsibility for distributing the huge body of Methodist writing and popular literature; and in 1753, the year when his daughter Philothea was born, every Methodist 'society' in the country was instructed to send orders for books to the Briggs' house at Hoxton Square[82].

The marriage of William Briggs and Elizabeth Perronet — Thomas Thompson's parents-in-law — had been conducted by Charles Wesley, who noted in his Journal on that day that "they seemed quite made for each other"[89]. The long friendship of the Wesley brothers with the Perronet family [see genealogical table] would make a study in itself. Briefly, Elizabeth Perronet's father was Vincent Perronet, Vicar of Shoreham in Kent for fifty eight years. Perronet's sons Edward (author of the hymn 'All hail the power of Jesu's name') and Charles were brave assistants to John and Charles Wesley in the days when Methodist preaching brought verbal abuse and physical assault[70]. The Wesleys made Vincent Perronet 'umpire' between them when they disagreed in their choice of Methodist preachers[23]. Vincent Perronet helped Charles Wesley to contract a happy marriage[89], and persuaded John Wesley into one which turned out badly[89]. John Wesley buried Charity, Perronet's wife[64]. Perronet's daughter, Damaris, led the Methodist 'society' founded by John Wesley in Shoreham[70]. It is John Wesley who records

how Damaris died, "literally of a broken heart", when her niece Elizabeth — sister of Philothea Perronet Briggs — was cruelly jilted[90]; but how that niece went on to marry Perronet's curate, who was also one of Wesley's preachers. Finally, Charles Wesley buried Vincent Perronet at Shoreham in 1785[23], and John Wesley's Journal movingly describes the end of the old clergyman's "holy and happy life"[90].

Those were the strongly 'Methodist' antecedents of Philothea Perronet Briggs, who in due course married Thomas Thompson in her grandfather's church in Shoreham. In the early 1770's, furthermore, when Thompson was still a young clerk in Hull and she was a teenage girl in London, she herself received nineteen letters from John Wesley which must undoubtedly have influenced her growing mind.

The letters — they survive in Wesley's printed correspondence, and are sometimes called 'Letters to a Young Disciple'[91] — were written from all manner of places where Wesley was travelling, and were addressed to 'Miss Phil Briggs' or 'Miss Philly Briggs'. The first letter, written in London in 1769, when the girl was sixteen, states that "You will want no help which is in the power of, dear Philly, yours affectionately, John Wesley". From Dublin, "You must learn to write sloping, not leaning upon your breast". Again from Dublin, "You may undoubtedly lose what God has given; but you never *need*. Let not the liveliness of your spirit lead you into levity. Cheerful seriousness is the point you are to aim at". From Galway, "Seriously and steadily, my dear maid, aim at [walking closely with God], and you will not be disappointed in your hope". From Kingswood, when she was ill, "Your present weakness will, I hope, be an unspeakable blessing. You were in danger of having more sail than ballast, more liveliness of imagination than solid wisdom ... Meanwhile you are to use all probable means of recovering your health. Taking many medicines, indeed, is not a probable means". A fortnight later, from London, "Perhaps youth, with abstinence from tea and whatever else you feel hurts you, may restore your health". From

The Rev Vincent Perronet, Vicar of Shoreham. Engraving printed in the Methodist Magazine, *c1790.*

Witney, "If you are writing any verses ... give me a picture of yourself. You may write in four-lined stanzas, such as those of the 'Elegy wrote in the Churchyard' ". (Gray's popular 'Elegy' had come out in 1750). From Leith, "You and I must be content with doing what good we can, and no more. Yet I love you for desiring to do more". And almost his last letter to her, from York in 1774, when Wesley was seventy and Thomas Thompson's future wife was twenty one, "Go on, trampling upon sin and Satan, and praising Him who hath put all things under your feet"[91].

The girl's father, William Briggs, excise official and book steward to the Methodists, also combined spiritual with practical advice in some notes written "To my dear Children" in 1772, when Philothea was nineteen. "Get wisdom from above in the management of your income", he wrote. "The most honourable life with regard to temporals is a good trade and employment. Don't live at Random if you can have a stated way of living"[4].

If a girl must combine "cheerful seriousness" with "a stated way of living", she could do much worse than to marry Thomas Thompson, and — although the statement cannot be verified — it is said[70] that John Wesley effected the introduction which led to their marriage in 1781. Meanwhile, of course, Thompson was working as a clerk in the office of Wilberforce & Smith in Hull — but also, in his spare time, as an evangelist in the surrounding countryside.

Forty years later, he described the state of rural Holderness in his young days. Poor communications were made worse by persistent winter flooding, and even in summer Holderness was isolated from the outside world. It was also, he said, an area of ignorant people, the majority of them illiterate, whose spiritual poverty was not relieved by the few educated men among them, the parish clergy. Against that depressing background, however, he wrote of how a number of people in the 1770s experienced conversion in Hull, and took the message of it into Holderness. He himself was one of those people. In the following passage, written in 1814, he refers to himself simply as "a young man"[1].

"In the year 1770 a young man, born and educated in Holderness, was brought by the providence of God to reside in Hull, where he had the opportunity of hearing the preaching of the Methodists, in a place called King Henry the Eighth's Tower [in Manor Alley], and subsequently in the preaching of the late Rev Joseph Milner, the Lecturer at the High Church or Trinity Church".

This "young man", Thompson went on, was now hearing the principal doctrines of the New Testament, and indeed of the Church of England, with new ears. At school, he had been "compelled, even to nausea, to repeat by rote Catechisms of various kinds; yet nobody had explained to him the fallen state of man, the consequence of sin, the necessity of repentance, or the way of salvation. He had never heard any serious conversation on these subjects in Holderness". Now he heard such 'conversation' in Hull, particularly in the vigorous preaching of Joseph Milner — who was, as a result, treated by many as "a man who preached strange doctrines, an enthusiast, and an enemy of the Church of England". In fact, Thompson explained, Milner preached the very doctrines of the Thirty Nine Articles which were printed in the Church of England's Prayer Book for all to see, but which were generally ignored.

Methodists, who at that time were likely to be members of the Church of England, as the Wesleys were themselves, were "plain men who declared the doctrines of the Gospel in plain language", wrote Thompson; and "the novelty of extempore preaching by laymen; the aptitude of address; the suitable language; and the intelligible mode of reasoning of those preachers brought multitudes to hear the Gospel".

Once a man in a local Methodist 'society' understood Christianity "experimentally" [i.e. through his own experience of it], and wished to preach, he was allowed to do so, Thompson went on. There followed, therefore, among Methodists in Hull, "a divine call to

Members of the Wilberforce and Smith families mentioned in the text

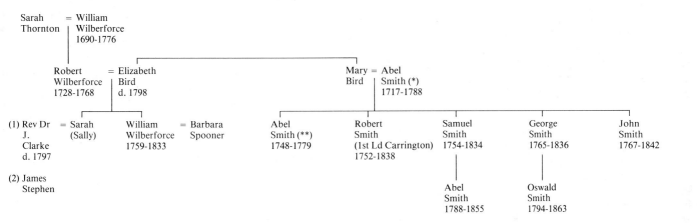

(*) Established the Hull bank, later Smiths & Thompson.
(**) Manager of Wilberforce & Smith, merchants, when
Thomas Thompson joined the firm in 1770.

Table based on Pollock, 'Wilberforce', and Leighton-Boyce, 'Smiths the Bankers' (see bibliography).

carry the Gospel into Holderness". He returns to describing his own part in it. "The young man before mentioned, who had come to Hull from that dark district, was eager to begin the work, and, in company with several of his pious friends ... went forth in the name of the Lord against the hosts of Satan. He has often travelled thirty or forty miles in Holderness on one day, and preached four or five times on that day, sometimes in houses and barns, and often in the open air". He and his colleagues "suffered abuse, in many instances, from mobs and wicked persons; but the Lord protected him from injury of every kind". He goes on to describe a "large and mischievous mob" at Skirlaugh, collected from many of the surrounding villages", which threatened to burn the house of John Duncan, where the sermon was preached, and used "sticks and stones" on the coach of Mr R. Terry and Mr I. Fox, from Hull, and on various poor persons who had walked from Hull on foot. (Skirlaugh is near Thompson's own home village of Swine, so the mob may have included his acquaintances). He describes, too, the violent opposition of the incumbent of Aldbrough; and how many of the inhabitants of Patrington "were only restrained from the most desperate conduct" [against the preachers] by the local magistrates. In each of those places, however, Thompson noted that the preaching had borne fruit. "One of the worst of the mischievous persons" at Skirlaugh had later travelled to Hull to ask forgiveness of a Methodist whom he had wounded. Aldbrough had, in due course, built a large Methodist chapel. Patrington had become, when Thompson wrote in 1814, the principal Methodist centre in Holderness. Nor was the increase in genuine religion the only result of the Methodist preaching. In Holderness, as in many parts of the kingdom, said Thompson, zealous preaching had, in due course, "promoted the increase of knowledge of every kind, and a general reformation of manners".

Robert Southey, the poet laureate whose biography of John Wesley[64] was not uncritical of the man and the movement, described the work of local preachers, such as Thompson was, comparing them with full-time ministers. "Many persons remained constantly in this humbler office, which neither took them from their friends nor interfered with their wordly concerns [as full-time itinerant preaching did]. They carried on their business, whatever that might be, six days in the week, and preached on the seventh ... Without their aid, Methodism could not have been kept up over the whole country ... and all that they received from the Society was a little refreshment at the cost of the people to whom they preached, and perhaps the hire of a horse for the day"[64]. Thompson, as a lay preacher himself, knew that the expenses were more than that. As he — the 'young man' — travelled about, he wrote, "his expences of various sorts were very considerable; but God restored to him tenfold, by the prosperity with which he was blessed in his business at Hull". Thompson saw the process as a circular one. God gives a man salvation. That man, if he is faithful, preaches it to others. God then gives the man what is best for him, which may be life, death, poverty or prosperity. And if God gives prosperity, that is one more thing of which the man must be steward, accountable both to God and to his business customers.

Thompson's mother died in 1777, and he buried her in Swine churchyard. Perhaps that left him free to pursue wider interests. At any rate, the next year he began a interest in overseas missions. He attended a particularly large Methodist conference in Leeds (over 2,000 persons took Communion at it); and it was the first at which the Methodists formally debated whether they should send Christian missionaries to Africa[82]. Thirty six years later, recalling the occasion in the 'Methodist Magazine' of 1814, Thompson wrote that several hours were given to the missionary debate, but that "the deepest impression seemed to be made, on the minds of all persons present, by the short speech of a young man, who appeared to be far gone in consumption, but who promptly offered himself as a missionary, and, in unaffected language, declared his readiness to go to Africa, or to any other part of the world to which it might please God and his brethren to send him''[82]. This 'young man' is thought to have been one Duncan McAllum of Dundee, whom John Wesley promptly advised to ''convert the heathen in Scotland'' instead[82] — but the incident was enough to impress itself on twenty four year old Thomas Thompson.

The heathen needed converting in England as well as in Scotland and overseas. Thompson continued to be a Methodist lay preacher in this country, and in 1807, in fact, was the first such preacher to sit in the House of Commons. Meanwhile there is a pleasant description of him at a much earlier date, probably between 1775 and 1785. ''Of the local preachers then in Hull'' (wrote a Mr Joseph Good, whose recollections of early Methodism in Hull are in the 'Methodist Magazine' of 1837), ''Mr John Spence, ironmonger, and Mr Thomas Thompson, banker, had been for some years distinguishable by their piety and zeal in preaching the Gospel. Mr Thompson had a particular attachment to Holderness, his native district; and he laboured there with perseverance, preaching in houses and in the open air, though he was often pelted by mobs, and treated with every kind of opposition. I remember that, when very young, I was much affected under [sic] his prayers in Manor-alley Chapel [opened in 1772]. A special influence seemed to accompany his confessions of original and actual sin, which were deep and touching. Like a child, I wondered how so good a man as Mr Thompson could have cause for so much lamentation. His preaching was of the most awakening and energetic character''[44].

It was, therefore, as an established Methodist lay preacher, within the Church of England, that Thomas Thompson married Philothea Perronet Briggs, daughter and granddaughter of Church of England Methodists, on 29th August 1781. The marriage was at Shoreham where old Vincent Perronet was still incumbent, though the service was conducted by a Mr Kennedy[61]. The couple, twenty seven and twenty eight years old respectively, settled in Hull, living at first at 17, Lowgate[28].

CHAPTER 2

The Thompson children and the Thompsons' Methodism
1781-1791

VARIOUS INTERESTING EVENTS TOOK PLACE in Hull at about that time. Success had crowned the efforts of the Hull Dock Company, and in 1778 the first ship had sailed up the river Hull, past Wilberforce & Smiths' wharf, to enter Hull's first dock — already England's largest, yet soon to prove too small. In 1780 young William Wilberforce, fresh from Cambridge and not wishing to go into the family business, entered Parliament with as yet no particular politics in mind[8]. Both regular and militia troops had been mustered throughout England in 1779, when France and Spain, opposing England in the American War of Independence, threatened invasion. This brought the West Norfolk Militia to Hull in 1780, and with it came its surgeon, Dr John Alderson, who settled in Hull and became one of its famous citizens. He married Sarah Isabella, daughter of Christopher Scott, a successful Hull merchant who had no sons and may well have left his money to his daughters[36]. John Alderson became the Thompson's doctor, and in due course one of his daughters married one of the Thompsons' sons.

The Thompsons' first child, Thomas Perronet Thompson, was born in 1783, and the second, John Vincent Thompson, in 1785. They were brought up under the steady, principled influence of their parents; and they were sometimes in the care of a servant, 'old Peter', who was "groom, valet and walking encyclopaedia" to them, and whose only departure from Methodist propriety, it seems, was his tendency to use the phrase 'Drat it!' when his pony reared[6]. In due course the boys went to Hull Grammar School, close to Hull Parish Church and to the site of the old prison, pulled down in 1792, where the debtor had taught their father Greek, Latin and French. There may have been money to send the boys to public schools, but Evangelicals feared that such schools might be haunts of vice[54]. In any case, Hull Grammar School was led by that respected Evangelical, Joseph Milner, who had come to Hull as a schoolmaster and had kindled young Thomas Thompson's personal faith. Joseph Milner and his brother Isaac, natives of Leeds, had achieved academic success largely through their own efforts[23]. Joseph saw at least two of the Thompson boys through school. Isaac, as President of Queen's College, Cambridge[*], saw three of them through university.

The Thompsons' third son, Charles William, was born in 1788. He may have gone to Hull Grammar School, but went on to a school at Boston Spa kept by a Mr Peers, who, like the younger William Scoresby, was first a whaling captain and then a clergyman[5]. A fourth son, Henry, was born in 1789, the year of the fall of the Bastille, but he only lived a short time[2].

In June 1790 John Wesley, eighty six years old, made his last visit to Hull. "Who can withold their surprise", the 'York Courant' had asked in May, "that, at such an age, this truly venerable man should be capable of the exertions he now uses?" Others described his simple, orderly appearance, smooth forehead and

(*) The College was at that period called 'Queen's', not 'Queens',' as it is today.

bright eyes[90]. Wesley's Journal shows that he spent a weekend in Hull, rising before 5 a.m., as was his wont, and following the routine which he notes economically as: 'Prayer; letters; sermon; conversation; business'. On Monday 28th June, his eighty seventh birthday, when he frankly noted that he was not nearly as well as he had been the year before, he records: "4 a.m. Prayed, sermon, prayer. 6 a.m. Chaise. 7 a.m. Cottingham, tea, conversation, prayer. 9 a.m. Chaise. 9.45 a.m. Hotham". And so on, preaching at Market Weighton and Pocklington before the day was out[90]. It is said that Wesley stayed with the Thompsons on that occasion, in a house at Beck Bank, Cottingham, which they began to rent in about the year 1787[25]. Perhaps he spent part of his Hull weekend there; perhaps he was just with the Thompsons that Monday for "7 a.m. tea, conversation, prayer".

Thomas Thompson was one of those who applied, in 1783, for the registration of a place of worship for the Cottingham Methodists[25]. The application came under the Toleration Act of 1689, which allowed "dissenting places of worship" to exist if suitable persons applied to the Archbishop of York or Canterbury for their registration. It is unlikely that most Methodists, at that time, considered themselves "dissenting" from the Church of England in the sense that Independents or Quakers were; but that was the procedure to be followed.

It is important now to explain how Methodism, and particularly the Methodists whom Mr & Mrs Thompson knew, related to the Church of England at that time. In July 1791, four months after John Wesley's death, Thompson wrote a letter to William Wilberforce which helps to clarify that question. In the letter, Thompson urged that the Methodists should stay within the Established Church. "I proposed to the Methodists here [in Hull], which was unanimously agreed to, to print and send, to all the Methodist societies in the nation, a letter declaring our determination to abide in connection with the Church of England ... and I hope it may have done some good. But still there is some weight in what is alleged in answer to our letter: 'At *Hull* your Ministers in the Church are men of exemplary piety, but we have none such in *our* town or neighbourhood' "[72]. That letter is probably the same as one mentioned elsewhere, in which Thompson told Methodists all over the country that if they parted from the Church of England they would form a "small, dry, separate party". They should reaffirm their loyalty to "Church Methodism" [sic], he said, "by refusing to have the Sacrament administered amongst us by the Methodist Preachers, or to have preaching in the Methodist Chapel here during the hours of Divine Service in the Church"[25].

Today, when the Methodist Church has long been a vigorous denomination in its own right, it is easy to forget that John and Charles Wesley, and very many of their early associates, considered 'Methodism' to be an invigorating movement within the Church of England. As late as 1787, four years before his death, John Wesley could write "I still think, when Methodists leave the Church of England, God will leave them. Every year more and more of the clergy are convinced of the truth, and grow well-affected towards us. It would be contrary to all common sense, as well as to good conscience, to make a separation now"[11]. By the time of his death he realised that "Providence" might lead the Methodists elsewhere[11]; but for him, the secret of Christian revival in England lay in seeking the co-operation of the Anglican clergy.

John and Charles Wesley were themselves priests of the Church of England, and many of the early Methodists found, with the Wesleys, that the sacrament of Holy Communion, as available in the parish churches (and not, at least until 1766, outside it)[64] played a vital part in their lives. Of course, the very energy of the Methodists, at a time when many Anglicans were lethargic, was bound to make Methodism seem a separate denomination. The Methodists' loyalty to the leadership of John Wesley; their ready attendance upon itinerant preachers; their membership of Methodist 'classes', or still more intimate 'bands'; their partaking in 'love feasts' (not a substitute for Communion, but readily misinterpreted as such by critics), 'watchnights', and 'covenant services'; all these smacked of a new denomination. Some Methodists, of course, wished to make themselves into one. Families were sometimes divided. (Within Mrs Thompson's family, for example, Vincent Perronet remained an Anglican clergyman invigorated by Methodism, but his sons Charles and Edward eventually found the Established Church too narrow for them, and left it). John Wesley, however, did not wish to separate; and others besides Thompson shared that viewpoint. Among them was Joseph Benson, who came to Hull as a Methodist in 1786, and was highly influential. Benson sought Anglican orders as a young man, was refused, and became a Methodist preacher; yet "was one of the old-fashioned type of methodist. He strenuously opposed the dispensation of the Lord's Supper in methodist chapels. He would have all partake in the church"[23].

In 1791 Wilberforce made his first motion in the Commons for the abolition of the slave trade, and was roundly defeated by 163:88, or nearly two to one[8].

The Thompsons' last child to survive, Philothea, was born in that year. Another daughter, Irene, was born in the following year[2], but a tablet in Cottingham church shows that she died young. Yet four children out of six growing to adulthood was quite a high proportion. Dr John Alderson, for all his medical skill, lost five children at an early age, and his wife Sarah followed them. Their epitaph in Sculcoates recorded it:-

'No single stroke the fell destroyer gave;
Five Children share their tender Mother's
    grave'[62].

CHAPTER 3

Smiths & Thompson's Bank
1784-1800

THOMAS THOMPSON WAS A MERCHANT and banker by
profession, and it is time now to give some account of
that work.

From the year 1787[7], two closely connected firms
shared premises at 25 High Street, Hull, now Wilberforce House. These were the merchant firm of Wilberforce and Smith, which had long traded from those
riverside premises; and the bank of Abel Smith &
Sons. Thompson worked for both firms.

Wilberforce & Smith, the Wilberforce family
firm, had been managed by Abel Smith II until his
death in 1779[54]. "After the death of an amiable young
man, Mr Abel Smith Junior, I was left in sole management of [that] large mercantile house at Hull", recalled
Thomas Thompson in later life[1]. Gordon Jackson
comments that "the prestige of Wilberforce & Smith in
the last twenty years of the eighteenth century was due
almost entirely to Thompson's astute business
mind"[36]. The partners in the bank, Abel Smith &
Sons, were Abel Smith the elder (1717-1788, father of
'Abel Smith Junior') and his other sons Robert and
Samuel Smith. None of those banking partners,
however, lived in Hull, so Thomas Thompson also
found himself in charge of the bank from day to
day[36]. He was assisted in that work by a clerk named
Cockerill[7], and later by more clerks. The bank was
prepared to be mobile, and Thompson and Cockerill
attended scattered customers and country fairs[36]; but
its base was at 25 High Street, and it operated from

there until it moved to Whitefriars in 1829[7], after
Thompson's death. Until 1828 it kept the accounts of
the Custom House next door to it in the High Street,
and was therefore sometimes known as the 'Custom
House Bank'[19]. An illustration in this book shows a
bank note depicting the Custom House.

In 1787 Thompson was taken into partnership both
in Wilberforce & Smith (merchants) and Abel Smith &
Sons (bankers). It was a mark of the Smiths' confidence
in him, which Thompson gratefully acknowledged[1],
that they lent him the money to buy his partnership[36];
and it was a relief to them, no doubt, that he was in
post, since Abel Smith, the senior partner, died the next
year[54]. His sons Robert and Samuel were occupied
elsewhere both as bankers and Members of Parliament[54]. As the partner resident in Hull, it fell to
Thompson, in due course, to 'live above the shop'. Mrs
Elizabeth Wilberforce, the slave abolitionist's mother,
still lived at 25 High Street, and the bank clerk on duty
slept in a room there on a rota basis[7]; but when Mrs
Wilberforce died in 1798, the Thompson family moved
into the house[1], and it became their home. By that time
the name of the bank had changed. The original name
of Abel Smith & Sons had changed to Abel Smith, Sons
& Co. when Thompson became a partner. It became
Smiths and Thompson in 1791, and remained so until
Thompson's death[7].

The partnerships and development of that bank, and
its associated business companies, are well traced in

13

Swine Parish Church in 1784. Thomas Thompson's parents were married here, he was baptised here, and his mother is buried there. From Poulson's History of Holderness *(1838).*

Leighton-Boyce's definitive work 'Smiths the Bankers, 1658-1958'[7], a book which traces the whole network of banks connected with the Smith family, of which the Hull bank was one. Its sections on Hull are largely based on the many ledgers and other archives of Smiths & Thompson's bank which were preserved by the National Provincial Bank in Hull[36] and are now in the archives of the National Westminster Bank in London. Those Hull records illustrate the general truth that banking, in the late eighteenth century, was an offshoot of merchant houses, though in fact any man or woman with money to spare could set up as banker to his or her neighbours[19]. At that time there were the banks in London (of which the Bank of England was one, but not yet unique); and the 'country' banks which served farmers, manufacturers and merchants outside London[19]. All banks in England and Wales were small, except the Bank of England, and were limited to six partners, since only Scotland had joint-stock banks before 1826[19].

A bank's assets included loans to customers; money deposited with agents in London and abroad; the partners' own money, often indistinguishable from the bank's; and the bank's own investments in government or other stocks[36]. A bank's services to customers were principally the safe-keeping of the customers' surplus money; short term loans of capital for business (as opposed to personal loans, which tended to be the province of money lenders); and the issue of notes[19]. Banks paid interest on money deposited with them, so that they could lend it out again, although the usury law, which continued until 1833, limited interest of any sort to 5%[7].

The use of bank notes began, in the late eighteenth century, with notes to individuals recording money deposited at a bank. They were hand written, bearing the depositor's name, the amount concerned, the date, and the signature of the banker. Such notes were for local use only, and were cancelled when returned to the bank[36]. However, as money came to move, increasingly, between the country banks and London[21], such

notes gained a wider circulation, and printed notes of fixed denomination came to take their place. One of my illustrations shows a draft of Abel Smith & Sons, dated 1788, with the printed name of Thompson among the partners, the symbol of the Custom House, and the signature of Thompson's clerk, Cockerill.

In the 1790s there were several established banks in Hull, among them Pease's bank, Bramston's bank and Sykes' bank[7]. (Thompson became a partner in the Sykes merchant house, and in 1814 recorded his "high respect for the family of Sykes, a name of the very first respectability in Hull . . . I have been a partner for many years with his family in a most extensive trade with Sweden")[1]. Smiths & Thompson's had regular connections with merchants in London, Yarmouth, Nottingham, Manchester and Thirsk. Abroad, the bank did business in Archangel, St Petersberg, Riga, Pilau and Königsberg[7]. Such a very wide spread of business favoured the development of printed notes; and printed 'Bearer' notes appear in Thompson's ledger as early as 1784[36]. The possibility of forgery of printed notes was therefore there before the end of the eighteenth century; and in 1795 a man called Spight tried to persuade an engraver at Gainsborough to forge Smiths & Thompson's notes. He was caught and "sent on board a Man of War"[7].

The war with France, which would last from 1793 to 1815, had a huge and obvious effect on finance. Early in the war the need to import, for example, grain and naval stores from the Baltic; the need to make remittances to governments and armies abroad; and the fluctuating situation in France itself, which made certain prosperous Frenchmen move their fortunes both into and out of Britain — all this led to unprecedented demands for immediate cash. This resulted in Pitt's Order in Council of February 1797, confirmed by Act of Parliament, suspending cash payments to anyone else and introducing a paper currency which, in the event, lasted throughout the war and up till 1821[19]. Thomas Thompson, as an established and successful 'country' banker, was invited to join the Commons Committee

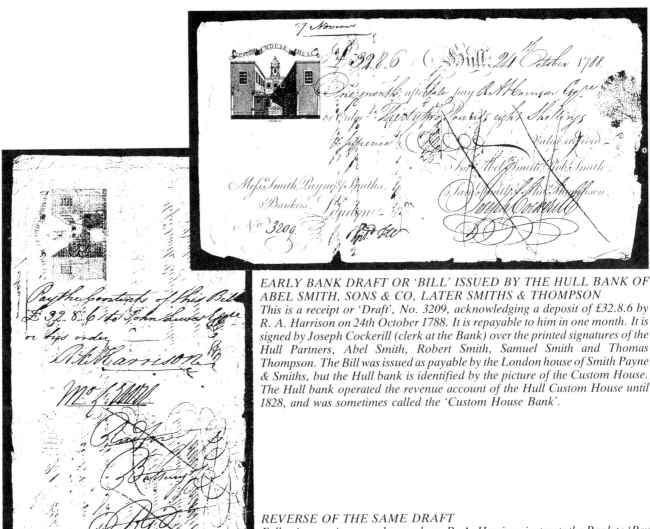

EARLY BANK DRAFT OR 'BILL' ISSUED BY THE HULL BANK OF
ABEL SMITH, SONS & CO, LATER SMITHS & THOMPSON
*This is a receipt or 'Draft', No. 3209, acknowledging a deposit of £32.8.6 by
R. A. Harrison on 24th October 1788. It is repayable to him in one month. It is
signed by Joseph Cockerill (clerk at the Bank) over the printed signatures of the
Hull Partners, Abel Smith, Robert Smith, Samuel Smith and Thomas
Thompson. The Bill was issued as payable by the London house of Smith Payne
& Smiths, but the Hull bank is identified by the picture of the Custom House.
The Hull bank operated the revenue account of the Hull Custom House until
1828, and was sometimes called the 'Custom House Bank'.*

REVERSE OF THE SAME DRAFT
*Following a quite normal procedure, R. A. Harrison instructs the Bank to 'Pay
the contents of this Bill, £32.8.6, to John Leurie (?) Esqre or his order'. John
Leurie (?) signs below ('Jno. Leurie') on receiving that amount from the Bank,
and the Bank crosses through the Bill, back and front, to show that the
transaction is complete.*

which advised on that Act. Speaking for Yorkshire, he told the Committee that those who would stick out for cash payments in gold would be the West Riding manufacturing districts, where small sums changed hands frequently; but that the agricultural areas would accept notes[7]. It was largely a matter of public confidence. If notes were required, Thompson, for one, would see that his bank issued dependable ones. Years later, as a Member of Parliament himself, he was found saying much the same thing.

No. 25 High Street, Hull (now Wilberforce House). Thomas Thompson's first place of employment, and his family's home from 1798.

CHAPTER 4

Holidays, tithes and poverty
1795-1800

IN 1795 MRS THOMPSON VISITED her widowed mother, Mrs Elizabeth Briggs, at Hoxton Square, and wrote from there to her sons Thomas and John, aged thirteen and eleven, at home in Hull[2].

"I am much obliged to my two dear boys", she wrote, "for their respective letters, which your Granmama [sic] saw and was pleased with, only she thought, as I did, that John had not taken much pains with his, which I could not help wondering it, as I believe he loves his Mother, and as he generally writes very neatly".

"Your friends have great expectations from you both", she went on, "which I am rather sorry for, as I had rather you should exceed their expectations than fall short of them. However, if you are only good humoured and obliging, and keep yourselves clean, and your hair smooth, we shall I hope do very well, for I dare say nobody will expect you to be Petit Maitres [sic] (if you are at a loss, you may look in the Dictionary for this term), but only to be civil, neat and orderly".

Thomas and John were to visit London, and their mother described how they were to see "the Museums, Abbey, Panorama, etc". "We have already planned an excursion on the Water with which I know you will be delighted", she went on. "It is to the Royal botanical Gardens at Kew, and in case that excursion should not afford us a sight of the royal Family, I shall inquire what is the best opportunity of seeing them elsewhere, as I should much wish you to see them, as Persons whom God himself has placed in so exalted a station, and who are of so much importance to us and all the Nation, as to demand our love and veneration".

She then reminds the boys that, "after all the pains your friends take to procure you pleasure, there will still be rainy days and vacant hours ... It will be impossible to set out in quest of wonders as soon as you are up, and to follow the chase all day. There must be intervals of comparative dulness [sic], and if you cannot be so philosophic as to bear these without vexation, you would, I am persuaded, be on the whole far happier at school". She suggests books and conversation, and that the boys bring "half a dozen good pens" and notebooks "such as Thomas has for his falconry", to fill up empty hours.

"I hope my dear Boys are very amicable together", she concludes, "and very obliging to the Servants, attentive to their Masters, and in particular very kind to their little Sister". She asks them to send Charles — presumably at school at Boston Spa — "a stone of biscuits if they can be got, and if his Master will not be displeased". "About the 20th of this month is the time I shall wish you to set out if it suits your Papa", was her final instruction, "but as that is uncertain, I hope you will not *tire*, but wait till he bids you prepare. I remain, my dear Sons, your ever affectionate Mother, P.P. Thompson"[2].

Papa — Thomas Thompson — was working that year on the first of his published books. He had been born in a village, and visited the countryside in the course of his work as a banker, so the subject was appropriate: 'Tithes Indefensible: observations on the origin and effects of tithes, with some remarks on the tithe laws, addressed to Country Gentlemen'. It passed through several editions[1]. His proposition was that "the imposition of tithes for the maintenance of the clergy — a burthen so reluctantly borne and so generally complained of — is clearly inconsistent with the principles of the constitution, and the propriety of the nation". It was no argument, he said, that tithes were instituted in the Old Testament and had existed in England for a thousand years: they had become a huge burden, and one which certainly did not improve relations between clergy and people. He set out very lucidly why tithes *were* such a burden, explaining that in the days of simple, hand to mouth farming, tithes were a simple tenth of a man's produce from his land; but that now, as the law stood, the tithe-owner claimed "one tenth of all the farmer's labour in the cultivation of arable land" — one tenth of what he laid out in wages, as well as on "enbanking, draining, fencing, manuring or in any way improving an agricultural estate". Out of £10 expended in labour, £1 went to the tithe-owner, "inasmuch as he engrosses all the beneficial effects arising from it". Furthermore, if a farmer spent money on improving his land, the tithe-owner claimed 10% of the additional produce arising from that additional outlay.

Tithes were uniquely a problem for farmers, Thompson went on. Very few *merchants* of the day, he said, would submit to pay 10% of their profits to the clergy. If in fact they did so, and made a 10% profit on a year's outlay of £5000, their tithe obligation would be one tenth of £500 (£50); but if a farmer used a capital of £5000 to cultivate his land, his tithe obligation would be £500. Thompson works out his argument in far more detail than this, and makes a considerable plea for the law to be changed. Little change, in fact, took place until 1836, when the Tithe Commutation Act changed the basis of payment. In the meantime, early nineteenth century Staffordshire pottery showed that others shared Thompson's views. 'Tithe Pig' pottery shows a scene of a farmer bringing eggs, corn and a piglet (a tenth of his year's produce) to a well-fed clergyman. Besides him stands the farmer's wife, with her tenth baby in her arms, asking the clergyman if perhaps he wants to claim the baby too[81].

Thomas Malthus was a contemporary who expressed views on the poor. Prior to his time, there was a tendency to equate a country's strength with a growing population. Malthus' 'Essay on Population' (1798) expounded the theory that because population increase geometrically (2,4,8,16,32), but food supplies only increase arithmetically (1,2,3,4,5), there would never be enough food for all. Man, because of his human passions, would always procreate, and therefore a perfect society with sufficient food for all could never exist. But at least, said Malthus in his second edition of 1803, society could discourage the poor from marrying when they could not afford it, and the individual poor themselves could "practise moral restraint" and postpone marriage till they could afford it. (Malthus was not in favour of birth control). His widely read works encouraged prosperous society in the view, which lasted well into the nineteenth century, that the promiscuous poor should improve their own lot by self-help, and should not be assisted too readily.

When poverty struck both town and country, however, the poor could not be held entirely to blame; and 1800 — the year in which Dr Alderson introduced smallpox vaccination to Hull — was a year of deep famine in Yorkshire. Food imports were restricted by the war, and two successive Yorkshire harvests, in 1799 and 1800, were disastrously affected by rain[88]. Industrial areas such as Leeds and Sheffield, where the working population no longer grew its own food, suffered greatly[88], and no doubt the same was true of Hull. Thomas Thompson was Chairman of the Hull Guardians of the Poor — 'Governor of the Poor', as it was locally called — in those two years. He was conscious of the burden of the poor rate upon those

PREFACE.

THOSE gentlemen who are acquainted with the expence of the culture, and the nature of the produce of their eſtates, well know, that TITHES in kind are a great deduction from the value of their property, and a conſtant impediment to the improvement of it.

THE effects of TITHES are at preſent much more ſenſibly felt and generally underſtood than in times paſt; but it is poſſible that, in the following ſheets, ſome facts relative to TITHES, may be ſtated in a more perſpicuous light than that in which the reader has been accuſtomed to view them. The ſubject deſerves examination, as it is of great national importance; and, in the midſt of a variety of mercantile purſuits, I have endeavoured to inveſtigate it with attention and impartiality.

THOMAS THOMPSON.

HULL, Auguſt 17, 1795.

Preface of Thomas Thompson's
Tithes Indefensible *(1795).*

who paid it, but also anxious to improve the conditions of the destitute[25]. Somehow or other, it seems, the poor rate was lowered by half, "Those who imposed on the charity were detected and exposed"[25]; and as a result, the Grocers Company of Hull presented Thompson with a silver plate "for introducing a system of oeconomy [sic] and industry into the Workhouse"[26], and the Corporation gave him the Freedom of the town[1]. But there was also outdoor relief on a very large scale. Soup kitchens were set up which served 4,000 people in Hull in January 1800[88]. A day of fasting and prayer because of the famine was held in March[54]. In May the soup kitchens served 6,000 persons, or one in five of Hull's population[88]. Soup distribution was unpopular in various parts of Yorkshire. People felt they were being given poor stuff; but it did save on stocks of cereals, and it did prevent further increases in the poor rate. Thomas Thompson, faced with a balancing act which few would envy, seems to have walked the tightrope courageously until the crisis passed. The next year he published his 'Observations on the Improvement of the Maintenance of the Poor in Hull'[24,25].

It may seem strange that 1800, a year of such want, was also the year in which Thompson bought the site of the house which would be called 'Cottingham Castle', and began to plant trees there, though building work did not commence until 1808, and the family did not move in until 1816[27]. Ill health, however, could strike at rich as well as poor. Hull was a smoky, grimy place. Mrs Thompson describes it as such in her letters, and was not the only person to do so. She suffered from illness, and it seems likely that nine year old Philothea already had the chest condition which shortened her life. So Cottingham, on a hill looking down on Hull, became the place where the Thompsons spent part of each year. The rented house at Beck Bank where Wesley may have visited them was replaced by another, identified as Southwood Hall (the house still exists) in Burton Road[28]. Mrs Thompson referred, in 1811, to living in a house in Hallgate with a "long green walk"[2]. Philothea wrote in 1812 that the owner of their house in Cottingham was a Mr Howarth[2] — and was perhaps writing of Beck Bank House, since that house was owned by Heyworths[28]. Local historians may identify what buildings they wish from these descriptions. Eventually, in 1816, the family moved into Cottingham Castle: but business went on at the bank in the High Street, Hull, and for some of each year the family lived in that old house as well.

CHAPTER 5

Beginning careers, and ending the slave trade
1802-1807

"Harrogate,
May 17th, 1802
Dear John,

The last time I wrote to you I was in so great a hurry that I could not give you an inventory of the things in the Museum, and therefore I send you one now".

So writes eleven year old Philothea, youngest of the Thompsons' children, in a beautifully penned letter to her brother John, aged seventeen and probably at Cambridge[2]. It seems likely that Philothea and her mother were at Harrogate for its waters and baths. Certainly they visited Ilkley, Hotwells (Bristol) and Bath for that purpose during the next few years.

The inventory of Philothea's Museum includes the following items. "A petrified bird's nest". "A nut of which the name and country are unknown, given by Miss Dikes". "A Cornish Diamond". "Four pieces of cloth brought in the 'Duff' [her father had a share in a ship of that name[28]] from Otaheite [Tahiti], with a piece of net made from the outside bark of a Cocoa nut". "A small piece of Sugar Cane given by Miss Ball". "Two Snake skins". "A box which opens in a curious manner, given by Thomas". A girl who lived in a seaport, and whose father traded abroad, might expect unusual items in her collection.

"We have had two letters from Thomas since he went", the letter goes on. "He was very well, but poor Watch [a dog?] was very seasick". Thomas, Philothea's eldest brother, had graduated from Cambridge and

hoped to join the Royal Navy as a midshipman, but he had first been sent on a voyage on the Hull ship 'Selina', which was partly owned by his father, to see how he liked the life[6]. He liked it, and spent two or three years of wartime service in the Royal Navy. It was the beginning of a remarkable career as sailor, soldier, colonial administrator, journalist, politician and inventor, which is described in full in his biography by Johnson[6]. His consistently down-to-earth character was shown early, when, in September 1805, at about the time he left the Navy, he saw Nelson walking down to the quayside at Portsmouth, through throngs of admirers, to set sail on the voyage which culminated in Trafalgar. Some of the onlookers knelt on the ground[51]; but Midshipman Thompson observed that Nelson had a face like a cod-fish[5]. The remark, perhaps, reflected the views of a family which would consider Nelson's victories as providential, but his liaison with Lady Hamilton as reprehensible.

Thomas Thompson the banker, meanwhile, was leading an active life. In the late 1790s, according to Jackson, he had administered Robert Smith's estates at Humberstone, near Grimsby, and at Wintringham, east of Goole[36]. There he had developed a theory of "three acres and a cow"[36], which now emerged, in 1803, in his publication 'Reasons for giving land to cottagers to enable them to keep cows'. 'Giving land to cottagers' would be seen in practice in Cottingham a few years later. In the same year, 1803, he produced a work on

Harrogate May 17th 1802

Dear John

The last time I wrote to you I was in so great a hurry that I could not give you an inventory of the things in the Museum, and therefore I send you one now.

In *j*orms a petrified birds nest, a piece of lead ore, a red white and green stone found in Robins Life Hole, four East Indian shells, one beautiful Margate shell, a piece of Derbyshire spar, a nut of which the name and country are unknown, given by Miss Dikes. A fine large Conch, a Cornish Diamond, two pieces of Mundic, one piece of bubbled Copper, a piece of Copper ore, Copper ore, Mundic, and spar in one piece, a small piece of needle tin, four pieces of cloth brought in the Duff from Otaheite with a piece of net made from the out side bark of a Cocoa nut, a small piece of Sugar Cane given by Miss Ball, Two Snakes skins & a boa which opens in a curious manner given by Thomas.

Some pictures & plans of the Cathedrals of Lincoln & Bath, & some pictures of the Roman pavement at Winterton, three views of an Ancient bronze helmet, & some pictures of antiquities sent by Papa.

One day last week we went to Knaresborough, and got a petrified Nettle root for the Museum. ~~Some Medallions coins & a Rice ear.~~

You see that our Museum is yet in its Infancy & therefore I hope you will contribute to it as much as you can.

My Cousin Sells is come to spend the Summer with me.

We have had two letters from Thomas since he went; he was very well, but poor Watch was very sea-sick.

Pray give my respects to Mr. Sowerby, & tell him I am very much obliged to him for his present.

Mama sends her love to you & wonders much at not hearing from you.

~~Aunt Jane sends her love to you.~~

I am dear John your affectionate Sister

P. Thompson

Letter from Philothea Thompson, aged 11 (1802).

French philosophers, in which he made clear his view that "if the influence of religion be removed from the minds of men, civil laws will be found utterly ineffectual for the preservation of order in society, and universal anarchy must ensue"[59]. Ten years earlier the government of France had officially abolished the Christian religion. Even in 1803, with Napoleon as First Consul, the Church in France only existed again because the State allowed it. It was quite reasonable for Thompson, banker and administrator, to believe that one function of religion was to promote a peaceful, orderly society, and to claim, from his own observation of France in recent years, that a godless society was a society of Jacobinism and of warfare.

The Thompson's second son, John Vincent Thompson (my own great great grandfather), graduated from Queen's College Cambridge in 1805, with the position of Senior Optime. He was disappointed not to be a Wrangler[5]. He made some effort to go into the Bank at Hull, but "as he found he was expected by his father to be early at the Bank to take down the shutters and sweep the place out, the young graduate very naturally objected. He chose the Bar as his career, and went to London, where in due time he became a well-known barrister"[5]. It was five or six years, in fact, before he went to London, during which time he seems to have studied law in York. A number of his mother's surviving letters are addressed to him at the house of "Mr Hanson, druggist, Petergate, York". The house adjoins what is now the York College for Girls. These letters mention John's legal studies; and it is possible that they were under an uncle. Thomas Thompson had a brother William, who was an attorney; the York directories of 1781 and 1784 (though not later) include a 'William Thompson, attorney'[10]; and Mrs Thompson's letters refer to John's "aunt" in York[2]. It cannot be definitely established, however, whether 'William Thompson, attorney' was Thomas Thompson's brother.

In 1806 Thomas Perronet Thompson transferred from Navy to Army, joining the Rifle Corps (95th Regiment) in time to take part in what still seems a remarkable episode. Cape Colony, South Africa, had been captured in January 1806. In April Sir Home Popham, commanding naval forces there, was apparently informed that Montevideo and Buenos Aires, in Spanish South America, would welcome a British expedition to liberate them. Although their independence was on Britain's agenda, no hostile action had been planned, and when Popham set sail with two British regiments on board, it was quite unauthorised by the British government. Buenos Aires was captured, however; the Spanish viceroy fled; Spanish treasures were despatched to London; and British merchants delightedly sent goods to Buenos Aires, a market previously denied to them by Spain. But then, to Britain's surprise, the people of Buenos Aires rose, and defeated the British troops which had so recently 'liberated' them. The Rifle Corps, Thomas Perronet Thompson with them, was among those sent out as reinforcements. He was captured and briefly imprisoned there, though then released, and he and his regiment were back in England by January 1808[8].

While he was abroad, two events took place which significantly affected the Thompson family. The Act for the abolition of the slave trade was finally passed; and Thomas Thompson entered Parliament. In the same year, 1807, Mrs Thompson made a memorable visit to Scotland.

The abolition of the slave trade had come slowly, blocked at every proposal; but finally, and almost prevented again by an impending dissolution of Parliament, the Act received Royal Assent in March 1807. Not everyone had wanted it. The vested interests were too strong. The existing slaves in British territories would not be emancipated until 1834, and Wilberforce himself believed that slaves must be trained for freedom. Nevertheless, the Commons concurred with huge applause when Romilly paid a moving tribute to Wilberforce, that day in March 1807, pointing first to Napoleon, at the height of his power and conquest, who must go to bed at night haunted by the blood he had spilt; and then to Wilberforce, who would "return that night into the bosom of his happy and delighted family, to lie down in peace and perfect felicity, conscious of having preserved so many millions of his fellow creatures"[3,54]. Within a few days, the African Institution was formed, with a wide membership of churchmen and politicians. It was to be "A Society ... on a very broad basis, for promoting the Civilisation and Improvement of Africa", wrote Wilberforce, who added that the Institution's work would make recompense for what Africa had suffered.

Thomas Thompson entered Parliament in July 1807.[79]. His nomination for Midhurst by Lord Carrington is described in the next chapter, as is his work to secure Wilberforce's election for Yorkshire.

Whilst the latter campaign was going on, Mrs Thompson set off on a tour of Scotland which lasted about nine weeks, which she recorded in a notebook of 46 pages, headed 'Observations in Scotland in the Summer of 1807'[71a].

"This little sketch of our Northern tour", the notebook begins, "is dedicated to my Philothea's amusement and pleasure. I shall therefore indulge in reflection, or confine myself to recital, as inclination may dictate". It was unusual for mere inclination to dictate anything in Mrs Thompson's well-ordered life; but the journey certainly seemed to provide her — and therefore her readers today — with a huge amount of interest. "We set out from York 10 May", she goes on; although from that day, for over two months, "we" travelled many miles without once being identified by name! There seem to have been two persons besides Mrs Thompson, and no doubt Philothea would know them. They could not have included Thomas Thompson, who was busy in York that May assisting in Wilberforce's election, although it seems possible that Thompson, anticipating his own entry to the Commons, may have asked his wife to make some of the enquiries in Scotland which she did.

Mrs Thompson mentions fifty five places in the course of the tour. It went northwards to Newcastle, the Borders and Edinburgh; on to Stirling, Perthshire and Blair Athol; south west of Glasgow and on to Loch Lomond and Inverary; back to Glasgow by another route, and south to Carlisle. The journey was 800 miles at the least, and there is only one reference to its difficulties. Two or three days after leaving York, the roads were rugged and heavy after much rain. "A prospect which in a fine day may appear delightful", Mrs Thompson observes, "will in a gloomy season lose all its charms. When a traveller is exhausted with fatigue, the garden of Eden itself might excite but languid admiration". After that, she complains no more. The party visited four ducal castles (at Daikeith, Blair Athol, Inverary and Hamilton); Heriot's School for boys, the Botanical Gardens and the new Bridewell prison in Edinburgh; the bleach yards, muslin works and potteries of Glasgow; a glass works at Dumbarton, but not Owen's cotton mills at Lanark ("Strangers are not admitted; the reason given is the great waste of time to the people employed"). Mrs Thompson seems to have gone everywhere with her companions, except when they climbed Ben Lomond and she did not — but she had the task, as the senior lady of the party, of climbing many flights of stairs in Glasgow to find them suitable lodgings.

Each Sunday in Scotland, the party attended the Kirk in the morning, and an Episcopalian or Methodist service later where one was available. Sometimes Mrs Thompson visited the sick, among them "Mrs A.D., a methodist of the old school, aiming at a heavenly life in a mortal body". She observed everything — their lodgings in Edinburgh (up seventy stairs), where there was "abundance of good pictures, but nothing was clean"; the funerals in Scotland, "which seem not to be considered as a religious ceremony"; the rich pelisses of Edinburgh ladies, contrasting with the "naked feet of the poor", but also with the economical habits of Falkirk, where "even decent, and sometimes smart women walk on the road with their shoes and stockings in a handkerchief". She describes both Lowland and

Observations on Scotland,
    in the Summer of 1807.

"Ignorance & astonishment are recipro-
-cal, & I am conscious that mine, are the
observations of one who has seen but
little."   Dr Johnson.

This little sketch of our northern tour
is dedicated to my Philothea's amusement
& information; I shall therefore indulge
in reflections, or confine myself to bare
recital, as inclination may dictate. We set
out from York 10. May, dined at Thirsk;
the Church of which Town is a venerable
Gothic structure, very capacious, & has a grammar
school adjoining. The church yard pleasant
with a stream of water, & a wooden bridge
on the side. a comfortable Inn, like an

26

First page of Mrs Thompson's Observations
in Scotland in the Summer of 1807.
BY COURTESY OF MR NIGEL HUGHES

Highland dress. She found herself kindly received by most people, and quoted a poor woman in Callander who bade her "Come into my house and drink some milk, *if it be your wull*". She particularly liked the Highlanders' manners, and when the mistress of an inn by Loch Lomond "appeared unequal to her station, though I believe she imagined herself above it", Mrs Thompson explained that the woman was really from the Borders. After church services she would record how far the preacher had "delivered the truths of the Gospel"; but she found reasons for those who failed, and for the congregations who failed their preacher. In one kirk the congregation showed "a degree of attention", but also "a striking want of solemnity. The most flagrant indecorum is the handing snuff boxes about. [But] perhaps much of what appears to us irreverent may proceed from reluctance to attribute sacredness to a *Place*".

It is a perceptive, enjoyable narrative: and although Mrs Thompson concludes it wistfully, "I wished much to have seen the Cairn Gorm, the blue mountain ... but I believe we did not travel in that direction", the reader does not notice the loss, having heard so much besides.

Mrs Thompson's Scottish journal has been preserved by one of her descendants. Another descendant has preserved a series of her letters dating from the same period; letters which colourfully illustrate some of the family's home life in Hull and in Cottingham. In November 1807, for example, she writes to John about the death of 'old Peter', the servant who had cared for the boys in their youth. A year or so before Charles had written to his mother to tell her that "Peter could not find the tickets at Cottingham, and must give bread loaves [presumably to the poor] from memory", and also that "Thieves are going about robbing Country-Houses. Peter is defended by a dog and a cat and a gun, and has not yet been attacked that I have heard of"[2]. Now Peter had died — "the good old man", Mrs Thompson called him. "I remember", her letter to John goes on, "Peter coming to tell me when Thomas's snakes escaped. 'Mistress! Edders getten away!' And when Thomas and you [John] had taught him to read words of three letters in Lambert's spelling book. 'Sure, never anybody did learn so fast!', he said, and then immediately gave up the attempt! The general savour of his humble piety, and friendly kind disposition, will long be remembered by me"[2]. In December 1807 Mrs Thompson writes, "Winter sets in early. My time is greatly occupied with poor clients ... I hope you [John], as a man of wealth, will remember the needy, who are likely to suffer more than is usual from the present deadness of trade". Mrs Thompson's letters are a mixture of present reality and hope in a better future. "The Carters have lately buried their youngest child William, a *very* fine boy about seven years old, whose high ambition seemed to be, to be Miss Thompson's man, and to ride behind her coach. Happy child, who has arrived at so much better a portion!"[2]

CHAPTER 6

The Member for Midhurst and his wife
1807-1808

THOMAS THOMPSON ENTERED THE House of Commons in the autumn of 1807 as Member for Midhurst, Sussex. Midhurst was one of the 'nomination boroughs' to which a man might be appointed, with little or no election, in the years before the 1832 Reform Act. Thompson's nominator was Lord Carrington, formerly Robert Smith, partner in Smiths & Thompson's bank. "I ought to pay my tribute of gratitude to the Family of the Smiths", wrote Thompson in later years; "and particularly to the present Lord Carrington, who, from the commencement of my acquaintance with him when he was one of the first Bankers of London, has not ceased to confer obligations upon me ... He has pressed me forward into notice, and into situations beyond my desires or my deserts"[1].

The fact was that Carrington had first-hand experience of Thompson's financial ability. He may also have been influenced, in his nomination of Thompson for Parliament, by his cousin William Wilberforce. Wilberforce had had much support from Thompson in the general elections of both 1806 and 1807. At the time of the 1806 election he noted, in his journal, the names of important men who met at York to promote his cause. "T. Thompson", he added, "said he was not of consequence enough to come, but [was] most active and kind, desiring to be put down for £500; but I was clear, subscription time was not till after victory on nomination"[94]. In the event, that election was uncontested; Wilberforce and Fawkes took the two

seats for Yorkshire, and Wilberforce probably did not take up Thompson's offer. The 1807 election, however, was a hard-fought one between Lascelles, Milton and Wilberforce. Thomas Thompson later wrote in his own journal: "I have always thought it an honour to enjoy the friendship of a man [Wilberforce] whose talents and piety deservedly place him among the greatest characters of the present age, and I have lost no opportunity of testifying my high esteem for him. In the last contested Election for the County of York, when Mr Wilberforce was elected [i.e. in 1807], I subscribed £500 towards defraying the expence of his election, and I lived eighteen days at York at my own charge, labouring in Committees, and in every possible way to secure his election"[1]. There is a contemporary account of nomination day at York in that 1807 election; and in view of the above information in Thompson's journal, Thompson seems to be the 'gentleman' mentioned in it. In that account, Wilberforce made his nomination speech. ' "It is impossible", said a gentleman, who rose as soon as Mr Wilberforce sat down, "that we can desert Mr Wilberforce, and therefore, put down my name for £500". This example spread; about £18,000 was immediately subscribed; and it was resolved that his cause was a county object'[94] [in other words that Wilberforce's friends, not Wilberforce himself, should defray the cost of his election].

It is not surprising, therefore, that Thompson was nominated for Parliament by Carrington, whether it was for his banking skills, or for the ideals which Thompson shared with Wilberforce.

Whoever the Member for Midhurst was, he need not know a great deal about his constituency. The right of voting had originally belonged to the owners of 120 'burgage tenements' outside the town of Midhurst; "the place where they stood", according to a Sussex guide book of 1831, "being now pointed out to the enquiring stranger by *120 stones*; so that the Members for the place have actually been the Representatives of so many blocks of granite, and have had neither property nor constituents to represent — the Patron's will being the only tribunal to which they need pay the least attention"[45].

Today that seems outrageous. Then, it depended very much on what a man did with his seat. Charles James Fox was Member for Midhurst from 1768-80, his father and his uncle having "bought the borough for their sons"[23]; and Fox was a highly active politician in national affairs. Palmerston began his remarkable parliamentary career in the same session as Thomas Thompson, succeeding his father in the pocket borough of Newport, Isle of Wight, and specifically instructed by its patron "not to set foot in the place, even for the election". Midhurst today has no record of Thomas Thompson's work on behalf of its blocks of granite; but Hansard's records of parliamentary debates carry at least thirty six of his speeches made over the next eleven years, fitted in during his work for the bank, for the Hull Dock Company, and for various aspects of religion and philanthropy — speeches which were on national issues, frequently illustrated by Yorkshire situations. Yorkshire was the county he knew; and his personal gift of £500 to William Wilberforce's election campaign that year had helped to ensure that Wilberforce was once again one of the Members for Yorkshire[1,54]. It should be remembered too, that he was the first Methodist lay preacher to sit in the House of Commons. Lord Carrington, he acknowledged, put "no restriction or even intimation as to the way in which he expected me to vote on any occasion", and therefore "in Parliament I have acted with a view to the best interests of my country; and in cases which related to religious liberty at home, or to the propagation of Christianity abroad, I have been united with those who have laboured to promote the good of mankind"[1].

Thompson's maiden speech, on 19th May 1808, was in a debate on whether there should be a fixed minimum wage for journeymen cotton weavers. Speakers both for and against the motion were agreed that that "respectable class of worker" did have "reasonable needs". Nevertheless, some opposed a minimum wage because it would force employers to discharge many workers through inability to pay their wages (something which would damage both the weavers and the 'parish' which would have to support them). The underlying problem, said others, was the lack of trade abroad due to the war. The proposal for a minimum wage was withdrawn. Thompson's brief contribution to that debate was to observe that minimum wages should be paid for a certain quantity of work done, not just for attending work[3]. Thorne's 'House of Commons, 1790-1810' records some of his votes and comments in the House in the next four years[79], but his next speech recorded by Hansard was not until 1812. It seems likely that his 'low profile' in Parliament during those four years was because his eldest son held a government appointment, and was also the cause of some controversy, as we shall see.

Mrs Thompson wrote to John in February 1808: "Thomas [John's elder brother] is in good spirits, and expects to civilise a good part of Africa. He and his father meet daily. Thomas is studying Arabic with great diligence. His lodgings are near Mr Wilberforce, on whom he calls 2 or 3 times a day"[2].

She was referring to the fact that, when Thomas Perronet Thompson had returned from Buenos Aires, in January 1808, he had had a long and enthusiastic discussion with William Wilberforce, as a result of which Wilberforce had asked the young man, still only twenty five, if he would let himself be nominated as Governor of Sierra Leone, the colony for freed slaves. The idea of such a colony dated from 1772, when Granville Sharp had pressed Lord Mansfield into the test case in which Mansfield ruled that there was no English law which allowed a slave owner who brought his slave to England, as many did, to exercise rights of ownership over the slave here. In 1787, four hundred and sixty 'free' negroes from England, and sixty white women from London, were settled in Sierra Leone, and later the idealistic Zachary Macaulay, father of the historian, became Governor there. However, for various reasons of climate, inexperience of the settlers and rapaciousness of their neighbours, the colony was not a success, and its management was now, in 1808, passing from the Sierra Leone Company, which was a child of the evangelical Clapham Sect, to the British government, which still continued to be much influenced by that Sect in its policy towards the colony[6].

Castlereagh, as Colonial Secretary, sent Thomas Perronet Thompson a formal letter of appointment in April, and the young man sailed from Falmouth in June, landing in Sierra Leone six weeks later, in circumstances described by Johnson and based on Thompson family archives. Before he left, he was already closely attached to a girl in York, who is described by two sources as outstandingly pretty[5,6]. She was Anne Elizabeth (Nancy) Barker, daughter of Thomas Barker of York, formerly Vicar of Nether Poppleton and subsequently Vicar of Acaster Malbis[12]. Nancy was recipient of a number of the young Governor's letters which have survived, describing his high aims in taking the post, his frustrations and setbacks, and his eventual recall to England.

At the time that he went, his mother, Mrs Thompson, was corresponding with her second son, John, in York. Many of her letters to John over the next few years have survived. Of her three sons, John was always accessible when his brothers were much further away.

I have the hymn book, 'A Collection of Hymns for the use of the people called Methodists', which Mrs Thompson gave to John in 1806, when he was twenty one. It is the collection published by John Wesley in 1779, in an 1804 edition. The hymns in it which are still popular today, though generally set to different tunes, include Charles Wesley's 'Love divine', 'And can it be', and 'O for a thousand tongues'; Isaac Watts' 'O God our help'; and Joseph Addison's 'When all thy mercies'. Many others would never be sung today. It is hard to imagine a modern publisher printing the hymn: 'Ah, lovely appearance of death! / What sight upon earth is so fair? / Not all the gay pageants that breathe / Can with a dead body compare' — yet the subsequent stanzas give a very real description of the release which death could bring to people without modern medicine or surgery.

Mrs Thompson's letters to John demonstrate her own belief in God's providence, and a wide range of other interests and concerns. In one letter, she asks John to recommend to Sir Walter Scott, through the medium of the 'Gentleman's Magazine', that Scott should write a poem on William Wallace. In January 1808 she describes a Welsh woman, a soldier's wife, who came "knocking at my parlour door" asking for help. Mrs Thompson had told her to go and find work, but then rebuked herself: "To recommend work to her when there was none to be had was little more than mockery". Work began on 'Cottingham Castle' that year, but there is a note of humour in both Mrs Thompson's and her daughter's letters when they describe their rather grand new home. "Your father caught cold, so the visit to the Plantations is deferred", writes John's mother in January 1808. And in May, when both John and his father were in London, "Please tell your Father that Richard has brought 46 Ewes and 52 Lambs, the cost of which is £57. I almost imagined we were going to resemble the Man of Luz [Jacob of the Old Testament], though I suppose our flock would be scarcely discernible on a Scottish range of hills. We propose visiting our Policy" — Mrs Thompson, recent traveller in Scotland, liked its word for the grounds around a large house — "as soon as the weather is more moderate". Commenting on a book which described Scottish justice as arbitrary and Scottish prisons as primitive, she writes "Were I to visit Edinburgh again, I certainly would contribute my mite of exertion towards the investigation of those evils''[2].

"Have you seen the curious anagram in one of the Hull papers, on the name of Napoleon Bonaparte?'', she asked John early in 1808. "I am not Classic enough to give the sentence rightly ... but I think it is 'bona repta pone lego', which is said to signify 'Lay down the stolen goods, you rascal'. I fear Bonaparte will not be disposed to comply''[2]. She knew that John would appreciate the witticism, but was perhaps too modest to say that she understood it — or had a husband and daughter who could. The proper anagram of 'Napoleon Bonaparte', 'bona rapta pone leno', gives the appropriate meaning: 'Lay down the stolen goods, you pimp', or perhaps, since Napoleon purloined thrones for his own family; 'you procurer'!

"Do you not rejoice that our dear Thomas is not to be killed on the Continent with the 95th?'', she wrote, in that year in which the Peninsula campaign began. She followed Thomas' fortunes in Sierra Leone, however, with a different apprehension. Her husband had had doubts whether ''the whole Sierra Leone scheme would end in delusion'', though he was reassured after talking with Zachary Macaulay[2]. Now she was aware that her son's outspoken, direct manner might offend the older members of the Clapham Sect. She was right: it did. Meanwhile, she wrote, "I trust a gracious Providence will overrule ... and either promote or disappoint his plans as will be for his real advantage in this world and the next. The African business, as it was intirely unsought, I hope to be a providential opening for usefulness, and I think it on all accounts preferable to the Army''[2].

As she thought of Thomas' close friendship with Nancy Barker, however, she was " ... less confident. The matter is at present in a very uncertain state, and if it will not be eventually for his comfort, I hope it will be turned aside. I should have expected your father would have made much stronger objection, but for myself I wish to be neutral''. Johnson, in his biography of Thomas Perronet Thompson, believed that the difference in wealth between Thomas Thompson, banker, and Thomas Barker, clergyman and father of Nancy, made neither party wish for the match. Mrs Thompson might claim to be 'neutral' in the matter. However, the friendship had arisen because Nancy's brother, also named Thomas Barker, Vicar of Thirkleby, north of York, had been a close friend of Thomas Perronet Thompson since their Cambridge days[6]. Mrs Thompson refers to Nancy's mother by her Christian name, Lucy, and mentions that Philothea had visited Thirkleby[2]. It seems, therefore, that the Thompsons already knew the Barkers quite well, which made the uncertainty about the future of the romance worse. Thus Mrs Thompson wrote urgently to John, after Thomas had sailed to Sierra Leone, asking for help. Thomas had arranged for a portrait of himself to be sent to Thirkleby, where Nancy was staying with her brother, and then on to Hull. "Cannot you, my dear John, contrive, without giving the smallest offence to any, to let the portrait come through *your* hands" — John had lodgings in York — "or in a way that no immediate communication might be made from Thirkleby? You know that I should be extremely sorry to disoblige any of your or your brother's friends, but circumstanced as I am, it is highly improper that I should hold intercourse in the present case. Do take some pains to save me from the real misery which most probably must attend this picture coming [directly] from Thirkleby''. It was the letter of someone trying to do her best for everyone, which seldom works. Perhaps, by the time she finished it, she had decided that providence would overrule. At any rate, she turned to more manageable matters. John had left a variety of clothing at Hull. "I wish I could have all your old shirts'', writes his mother, "that I might *mend* some and *end* others''![2]

31

CHAPTER 7

Crossing the river
1808

NOT SURPRISINGLY, THOMAS THOMPSON is often described as busy at this time. He was an active and successful business man, and had now taken on a Membership of Parliament at a time when issues of both war and peace must be decided. In December 1807 Mrs Thompson wrote to John, "Your Father has not been quite well, from attacks of his old complaint. He is likewise very busy as usual"[2]. In January 1808, "We were to have gone to Cottingham last week, but your father made a Bride visit where the room was very hot, and he got cold". The next month he was in London, where he was anxious about the Sierra Leone proposals, which concerned him both as a member of the Africa Institute and as father of the proposed Governor. "I scarcely ever knew your Father write in a more desponding tone", writes his wife; "he was tired of Parlt. — of London — almost of everything". The next month he was expected in Hull: "Your Father talks of visiting us in the next week, but you know how uncertain he is. He describes himself as being in a constant bustle, having scarcely time to command half an hour for his own purposes". But a fortnight later, "Your Father and the letters came in this morning together. He seems pretty well, but looks a good deal *fagged* [sic]. He travelled in the mail coach, which he has often resolved against — and the passage over the Humber was in a sort of minor squall"[2]. In addition to all this, he was a Methodist lay preacher. The rota of the Hull Circuit, 1808, shows him preaching once a month — at Scott Street in May; at Newland in June; at Drypool in July; at Stoneferry and Drypool in August; at Waterhouse Lane in September; and at Anlaby, Hessle, Little Weighton and Cottingham in October[25]. As has already been shown, this Methodist preaching was supplementary to his support for his local parish church.

The Thompson's third son, Charles, had entered Queen's College Cambridge in 1805. It was probably in the following year that he wrote the letter from Hull, already quoted, in which he described 'old Peter' on guard with "a dog and a cat and a gun". Only part of the letter now exists, beginning rather abruptly with Charles' advice to his mother "... take time to see every body in London, as it is of no consequence whether you get to Birmingham in February or March. If you want the *needful* [sic], my Father says that he will send you fifty Pounds from Hull, although the Loan is still a bad job, and a Flax dresser has broke and is gone to York Castle [i.e. to York prison as a debtor]"[2]. He goes on to say that "The Hull lads have done no wonders this year at Cambridge", though he himself was a successful scholar, as all three brothers were. In December 1808 Mrs Thompson mentions him, presumably at Cambridge: "Charles writes in very good humour, and seems satisfied with his success thus far"[2].

Philothea, the Thompson's daughter, was by then a girl of seventeen. Both she and her mother had chest complaints. Mrs Thompson wrote in November 1808 that she was consulting Dr Alderson since the family insisted, but "maladies of the lungs do not yield to medicine". "Nor do they indicate danger in subjects of half a century", she went on (she was fifty five years old) "as they do in persons under half that age". That summer Philothea had been to Ilkley for her health, on the direction of the Leeds physician Mr Hey. Mrs Thompson's niece Charity Gray had come to visit the Thompsons in Hull: "A very nice girl she is", wrote Mrs Thompson. "We mean to have a party of young scholars to see the Magic Lanthorn [sic] whenever you [John] will come and exhibit for us". So Charity went with Philothea to Ilkley, and Mrs Thompson visited there too. "I assure you Ilkley has many beauties — a fine river winding through it, fine walks and shady groves", was her description, written in the hope that John would visit them all there[2].

But death never seemed very far away. The Thompson sons' total of eleven years at Cambridge (Thomas 1798-1802, John 1801-1805 and Charles 1805-1809) had almost spanned the years when Thomas Sowerby was tutor at Queen's[99]; and Mr Sowerby died of consumption, that summer of 1808, aged thirty four. He had been a friend of the Thompson family, and a contributor to young Philothea's 'museum'[2]. "Little did I think, when the amiable man took leave of me at the Coach door in High Street three years ago last Easter — all vivacity and friendliness as he was — little did I then think we were to meet no more!", wrote Mrs Thompson. A letter from John had been the last which Mr Sowerby received before he died. She took it very much as a challenge that all who knew Mr Sowerby should follow the young man's Christian example. In the same month they "rang the passing bell" for Mr Thurlwell, Vicar of Cottingham[2]. Mr Thurlwell had at one time pressed, with Thomas Thompson's support, for greater observance of the Lord's Day in Cottingham[28], but latterly Mrs Thompson had commented that it was only a sense of duty, and her veneration for the Church of England, which had kept her at the parish church, where things were "intolerably muddled through"[2]. Now Mr Thurlwell had died, and was buried inside Cottingham church one Sunday morning, "just in front of the reading desk, in a walled inclosure [sic] the size and shape of the Coffin. It was slightly covered with earth and sand", adds Mrs Thompson, "but being the Sabbath, had not been bricked down — all of which added to the solemnity"[2].

It was Mr Sowerby's death which prompted Mrs Thompson to tell John how happy she would be if he could be a clergyman. Referring again to the Cambridge tutor, whom she called "the valued saint now departed", she wrote to John: "It has sometimes risen in my mind that it is possible that his mantle might descend upon you, and that you might step into his vacant sphere as a minister of Jesus Christ. ... I will *never* urge this point, but as the fond and favourite wish of my heart, you will forgive the suggestion, and the indulged hope, so long as you are not fixed in other stations"[2]. I have found no evidence, however, that John ever considered ordination.

CHAPTER 8

Africa, Malta and the Duke of York
1808-1809

THOMAS PERRONET THOMPSON'S CAREER in Sierra Leone lasted less than two years. The detail is in Johnson's biography[6]. Briefly, on his arrival he gave more recognition to African chiefs than had been expected; he exposed, and rejected, in that colony for freed slaves, an 'apprenticeship' scheme which was itself a form of slavery; and he did not report the situation diplomatically to England. As a result the Clapham Sect, more than the British government, felt that he had exceeded his authority, and it was arranged for him to be replaced; though until his replacement arrived, the young Governor worked against time to improve his colony.

It was an embarrassment for Mr & Mrs Thompson. They were friends of Wilberforce, who had given their son this opportunity while still a young man. They were financial supporters of the Sierra Leone project: the Bank in Hull held stock in the Sierra Leone Company[7], and Thomas Thompson was a subscriber to the Africa Institute. Their Christian faith linked them with the zeal of the Clapham Sect, in and out of Parliament; and Thomas Thompson was a member of that Parliament which administered Sierra Leone. Thus they were mortified that their son had not shown due gratitude to older and more overtly 'Christian', heads, but had arrived in Sierra Leone and had governed there as he saw fit. Had Mr & Mrs Thompson been able to see it, their son had really put the ideals of the founders of Sierra Leone into practice, out there where few of its

founders had ever been; but at the time they could not see it that way. Thus Mrs Thompson wrote to John in October 1808, "Mr Stn. [probably James Stephen, married to Wilberforce's sister] speaks very kindly and cordially of 'our young Governor', but fears that he has been premature and hasty ... He approves however the principles and energy by which things have been conducted. He says, 'Your son was angry at these transactions. *He was right*. He set the captives at liberty. *He did right*'; and proceeds to say how greatly the confidence of the poor African must be increased in the favourable disposition of England towards them, when they see the ardour with which the new Governor espouses their cause. From all this'', Mrs Thompson goes on, "it should seem that we have not so much to dread as we had apprehended ... Since then a letter has arrived from Mr W[ilberforce], which says 'The only thing which excites apprehension in me, is his [Thomas Perronet Thompson's] seeming disposal to trust too much in his own judgment, and to hear with too little deference the opinions and characters of those who differ with him ... May it please God to preserve and direct him, and above all to inlighten and sanctify him' ''[2].

The autumn of 1808 was a time of despondency for Mrs Thompson. She was worried about Sierra Leone. After the summer visit to Ilkley — which she, Philothea, and various visiting relatives seem to have enjoyed — she did not like the winters. She remembered another of her children, Henry, who had died as a baby nineteen years before — "lent to us for a season", she writes "... it is a pleasing thought that we shall soon be restored to those who are gone before us". How happy she was, therefore, when the new Vicar of Cottingham, Mr Deans from Aberdeen, stayed with the Thompsons before moving into "the little cottage in the church yard", and proved himself "*sound* and *solid*"; and when Mrs Deans sang them a Scottish song which brought them "almost to tears". The song was 'The land o' the leal' (land of the faithful, or heaven), written not long before by Lady Nairne for a friend who had also lost a baby.

'I'm wearing awa', John
Like snaedrifts in the thaw, John
I'm wearing awa' to the land o' the leal.
There's nae sorrow there, John
There's neither cauld nor care
The days are aye fair, in the land o' the leal'.

She copied it out, down to the last stanza, 'Then fare ye well, my ain John'. How lovely for Mrs Thompson that almost every line of the song ended with the name of her favourite correspondent, John. That day she signed her letter to him, "Then fare ye well, my ain John, from your ever affectionate Mother, P.P. Thompson".

A few of John's letters to his mother have survived, among them a humorous one sent to her in Ilkley in October 1808, almost certainly describing a visit to the Thompsons' rented house in Cottingham by one of Thomas Thompson's partners in the bank. (Thompson was the only partner who lived in Yorkshire). "The Master and his accompaniments", wrote John, "have just taken their departure in a Coach and two. If ever you saw the horses that draw Pidcock's Elephant give the strain at first setting off, you may have some idea of the exertion necessary for two horses ... to put an equal strain in motion. We have had some difficulty in doing the honours today, as my Father and I were alone in that duty. My Father began in the morning by pulling the Sofa Cover back, that none of the white might be seen, and whilst we were attending to other similar minutiae, our fire settled into one of those beautiful heaps of brown ashes topped with black coal, which now and then greet you on your entrance into an Inn, on a winter's morning, when it is too late to go to bed and too early to get any breakfast. [As we tried to poke the fire] we heard a talking as of various confabulators approaching ... the parlour door opened... It would be tedious to mention all the formalities which took place before everyone was seated". And so on, until the guests departed, 'like Pidcock's Elephant'[2].

This letter was enclosed in a means of postage available to Members of Parliament and certain other officials; a 'frank', or free wrapper. The frank of this particular letter bears Thomas Thompson's authenticating mark 'Tho.—free—Thompson'. The frank of the letter sent to John on another occasion, and illustrated in this book, is authenticated 'Free. Tho. Thompson'.

In the next year, 1809, we hear more of Charles William Thompson as he leaves Cambridge. A niece, Isabel Sidgwick, wrote of Charles many years later: "He had the military fever early, and practised all manner of hardships at College, lying on bare boards and in everything imitating the manner of his hero Charles XII of Sweden. ... [He was] headstrong, rebellious, and full of a kind of mischievousness then in vogue"[4]. On graduating he was awarded a Travelling Fellowship, with which he visited Malta and Egypt. The condition of the Fellowship seems to have been that the holder should describe his travels in Latin to the Vice-Chancellor. At any rate, three letters from Charles Thompson to the Vice-Chancellor survive in the Cambridge University Library, two from Malta and one from Egypt, written between June 1810 and April 1811[68].

These letters are significant because they describe recent events during the Napoleonic wars. Sitting in Valletta, Charles describes, in Latin, how Napoleon took the island from the Knights of Malta (1798), how the British helped to restore the rule of the Knights (1802), and how the people of Malta then chose to have the British to rule them. Sitting in Memphis, south of

35

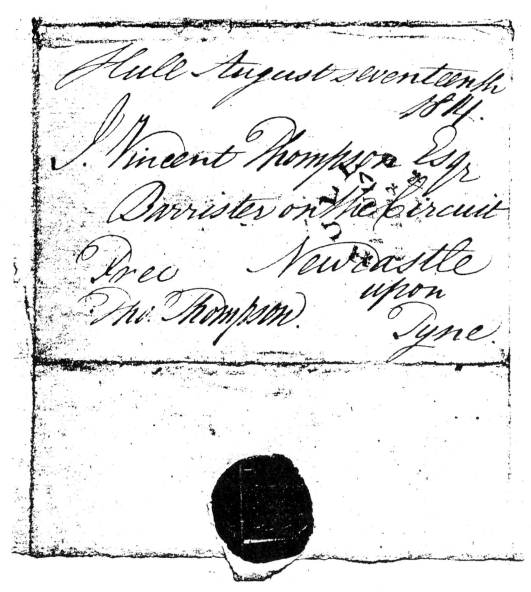

Postal 'frank' of Thomas Thompson, with his signature, addressed to his son John, 'Barrister on the Circuit' (1814).

Cairo, he describes, in Latin, how Napoleon defeated the Mamluks (also in 1798, after taking Malta), was in turn defeated in Egypt by the British (1803), and how Mahomet Ali had very recently taken power by massacring the Mamluks (1811). The letters are each twenty pages long, and the Travelling Fellow ends one of them humorously. "Sed quid ago? Quo progredior? Quae erit finis? Hic quidem liber est, non epistola". ("But what am I doing? Where am I getting to? What will be the end of it? This really is a book, not a letter!"). He signs the letters 'Baccalaureus Peregrinans et Signifer Anglo-Siciliae Centurio', the latter designation, 'Ensign of the Anglo-Sicilian Regiment', denoting his recent commission in the Sicilian Regiment of Foot. (My speculation is that this regiment was formed when Napoleon, in 1808, placed his brother Joseph on the throne of Spain and his brother-in-law Murat on the throne of Naples. This expansion of Napoleon's dynastic power into Spain was a direct cause of the Peninsula War. When Murat took possession of the Kingdom of Naples he did not occupy Sicily, which was part of that Kingdom, and Sicily may then have formed this anti-Napoleonic force.). Charles Thompson was not complimentary about his Sicilian soldiers. They had been recruited from the hospitals, galleys and prisons of Palermo, he told his father in 1810, and "in consequence, all the able-bodied men were felons, and all the well-disposed were halt or blind"[6].

Charles was not yet in the Peninsula, where he would later go with the Grenadier Guards, but Hull got its own news of that campaign. "A brother of Lord Mahon's was killed at Corunna", Mrs Thompson wrote to John in January 1809: "we suppose it to be the youth who was with T.P.T. in the 'Isis' ". (Lord Mahon was Member for Hull, and married to Lord Carrington's sister[54]. The 'Isis' was the ship on which Thomas Perronet Thompson had served as a midshipman)[6]. "Dr Alderson, I know, is in great anxiety for his son, who was with the Troops in Spain. He was a Surgeon, and on board the hospital ship, but in the closing scene would probably be exposed the same as the rest". (This son of Dr Alderson would not be the well known James, later physician to Queen Victoria but then only fifteen years old: it would be Christopher, who was later a surgeon at Waterloo). Finally, among Mrs Thompson's news that day, "My poor friend Mrs Wyddere must likewise be much distressed, as her eldest son was with the Dragoons there".

In 1809 John spent some time studying at Edinburgh University. He compared it very unfavourably with Cambridge, though he was delighted by the far-ranging lectures of Dugald Stewart[2,23]. He wrote from Edinburgh to his father at the House of Commons, at the time of the 'Duke of York affair' of 1809. The Duke, whose lofty statue gazes down today on processions in the Mall, was an efficient commander in chief of the Army. His mistress, Mrs Mary Clarke, whose striking face adorns the Regency Room of the National Portrait Gallery, was brought before the House of Commons for selling numerous commissions in the Army to the highest bidder. The question was whether the Duke had also received money from these transactions. It was decided that he had not, but he resigned his command — though he was soon reappointed by his brother, the Prince Regent. It was during the early part of the House of Commons enquiry that John Thompson wrote this letter to his father, in Westminster, about Mrs Clarke: "The woman is, as Joseph Milner [headmaster of Hull Grammar School] used to say, a harlot, but the very nature of the business supposes her to be so". And he goes on to give a vignette of the House of Commons as it then was; the old House, before it was destroyed by fire and rebuilt as we know it today. "When you begin to see the boats on the Thames through the window behind the Speaker's chair, I think it not improbable that you will agree with Mr Fuller, 'That Gentlemen had better get to bed and go to sleep' "[2]. Mr Fuller, MP, had recently made that remark in the House; and I take it that John Thompson, in quoting him, was recognising the fact that his father, the Methodist Member, would rather be at home than listening to the tale of Mrs Clarke's amours. But I was also interested in the "boats on the Thames", and recently ascertained that in the old House of Commons there was indeed, behind the Speaker's chair, a way down to the boats on the Thames, and that at the cry 'Who goes home?', Members would gather in groups for safe passag through the fields to the City of London, or to share th boats which could take them home by river[34].

The House of Commons by K. A. Hickel (1793). The picture shows the old House, where Thompson sat from 1807 to 181

CHAPTER 9

A fitting life for Philothea
1809

THE THOMPSONS OFTEN SENT BOOKS or newspapers to one another. In November 1809 John asked his sister Philothea to send him something, and her reply describes the scene at Cottingham. "The night I received your note, Papa was writing for the [Methodist] Magazine as usual, and I hoped he was deeply interested in him employment, but alas! he interested himself so much in the packing of the parcel for *you* without delay ... that I could scarcely obtain permission to warm my fingers before I took brown paper, pack thread and what not [sic] to finish this official dispatch. Could I have *scribbled* on a *Slate*, you would have had a dispatch something resembling that of the African Secretary, but pen, ink and paper could not be very easily employed in my chimney corner". She and Papa' had been to see the new trees planted in neat rows in the grounds of "the Chateau", and Papa had laughed to see how the gardener had planted "the little dark shrubs, I forget their name, in a row like rifle men on parade". Because of Papa's own precision, however, the "great Gate" must be altered: its proportions, he had told Philothea, were not correct[2].

Philothea tells John of an incident in which she and her aunt — probably Miss Jane Thompson, Thomas Thompson's sister — had gone to a silversmith, Mr Jones of Hull, to buy a table knife. Mr Jones had brought out a drawer of pearl jewellery, and although Philothea had said she did not want any, Mr Jones said he would notify her when his new stock came in.

"About a week later", the letter goes on, "my Father returned from Hull in the Coach with a very genteel young man", and ushered the young man into the parlour for Philothea to look after. "The youth opened a little box, and to my horror I beheld the most beautiful Pearl ornaments, of all sizes and descriptions". Philothea had neither money nor inclination to buy the pearls. "Papa strolled in *by accident*", but he only laughed. So, "I requested Mama to make a speech for me, which she did, and I came off *tolerably* well. Now was it not a misery? I was vastly inclined to cry about it". But perhaps she had just written all this to entertain her brother. "Voila!", she writes on the next line, "my paper is finished"; and she signs her name, "Your most affectionate sister".

Philothea is an intriguing person. My initial information about her suggested a quiet, scholarly girl who stayed at home. She did stay at home for the most part, but emerges with just as full a character as her brothers Thomas, John and Charles, who had far wider opportunities.

There is no doubt that her parents had strict ideas about her upbringing. Mrs Thompson wrote in 1808, when Philothea was seventeen: "I am sorry an idea has got abroad that Philothea is to be *kept up* till she is nineteen, and more so as it is a natural deduction that she is then to *come out* ... I could wish to shelter her for a year or two longer, that she might attend to her own improvement. I hope she sees the importance of improving time and opportunity, and will be guided aright... Certainly a life of visiting is not often a life of improvement"[2].

Her brother Thomas wrote to his future wife Nancy, at about that time, that he would not wish Nancy — who had been at a boarding school in York — the sort of education his sister Philothea had. "Her education, whether properly or not I do not pretend to say, has been much more that of a man than of a woman, and she has studied the classics till I dare say she has contracted a predilection for their style and peculiarities"[2]. Philothea's niece Mrs Sidgwick, writing many years later, describes Philothea's note-books and schemes of daily study: "too many slices, I think, to make a good whole". The girl studied "several languages, a little music, a little painting, and much reading of literature"; and she did painstaking and beautiful lettering and calligraphy[4].

Perhaps it was not all serious. Philothea's mother wrote once of her daughter "playing away vehemently" on the piano, and of her niece Charity, on another occasion, "jabbering away in broken French"[2]. Nevertheless, the general principles of 'improvement' were there. They were very much those of Hannah More, the blue-stocking whose books of religious and moral precepts had great vogue at that time. Mrs More's extremely popular novel 'Coelebs in search of a wife' — a description of a young man's quest for an ideal partner in life — came out in 1809. The young man Coelebs, or Charles, is advised by his mother against "the captivating exterior of any woman who is deficient in sense or conduct"[47]. He his advised by his father against "the exhibiting, the displaying wife", and urged to seek "the informed, the refined, the cultivated woman". The young man himself decides that his wife must be "elegant, sensible, prudent, well-informed, well-bred and pious". Philothea's niece Mrs Sidgwick, writing in the late nineteenth century, called him a "prince of prigs" for that attitude; but Mrs Thompson, writing in 1809 when the book had just come out, said "I am so much pleased with Mr Calebs that if his

counterpart were to come this way ... a few years hence, I should have great pleasure in entertaining him hospitably"[2]. By contrast, she wrote of her cousin Mrs Amelia Opie, another author of improving stories "I believe Mrs Opie is in Hull". (Amelia Opie visited her widowed uncle, Dr John Alderson, in that year acting as hostess at a large ball which the doctor gave[16] "Mrs Opie is a very intelligent and unassuming woman ... but exceedingly gay, and some of the sentiments in her tales I think very objectionable. Her Girls [in her tales] seem invariably to *fall in love*, and need very little *wooing*"[2]. So Philothea had little freedom of choice of action: yet in spite of it, she comes across in her letters as a warm, humorous person.

The Thompsons make little or no reference to Christmas — whether the 'old Christmas Day' on 5th January or the modern 25th December — apart from mentions of "seasonable greetings". (One difference between John's hymn book and more modern publications is that the former offers only one Christmas hymn, preferring to mark Good Friday and Whit Sunday). On 25th December 1809 Philothea wrote about her mother's health. "Mama's cough is not any better than it was, but she is now trying that most awful of cures, a blister, which I hope will have the desired effect. I think from all accounts, I should bear a great deal before *I* could submit to such penance". When 'Mama' wrote to John the next Christmas, on 24th December 1810, she did not refer to health, but she did write to him on half a sheet of paper, responding to a very short letter from him with that very small one of her own. In it, she made a plea for all those who stay at home, and thereby lack the stimulation their children enjoy. "In reply to your observation of not having heard from me for these six weeks, I never conceived it to be incumbent on the party *staying behind* to write first ... The party removing goes into new scenes, and must have materials for a letter more easily than the person staying at home. This being premised, I am willing to take your ten short lines as *breaking the ice*". Isolated as she often felt, however, she was concerned for others too. John's manservant Richard travelled with John, and was sometimes the bearer of letters and messages. "I hope Richard keeps his Master's boots and shoes waterproof" writes Mrs Thompson; but also "I hope your man Richard is not demolished by his wet journey to York". She asks John "to hold himself in some sort responsible for Richard's morals" when Richard meets "worthless Lacquies [sic]" at hotels; and she adds, after one of John's journeys by coach, "It is well they threw no Trunks or packages in the Boot [of the coach] while poor Richard occupied it"[(2)].

Dr John Alderson.
The portrait in Wilberforce House.
BY COURTESY OF HULL CITY MUSEUMS
AND ART GALLERIES

41

CHAPTER 10

Spa towns and a runaway marriage
1809-1811

THE DUKE OF PORTLAND, Prime Minister when Thomas Thompson entered Parliament, resigned in October 1809, and died a few weeks later. During that difficult year Moore had won the battle of Corunna, but had lost his life there. The 'Duke of York's affair' had been investigated. Wellesley, later Duke of Wellington, was victorious at Talavera in the Peninsula, but had to retreat through lack of support. Napoleon defeated Austria. A major expedition to Walcheren under Lord Chatham failed miserably, and the Foreign Secretary, Canning, duelled with the Minister of War, Castlereagh, over it. Burdett's motion for parliamentary reform took him to the Tower, and raised the London mob to bring him out of it. In that mood of national uncertainty it was hard for Spencer Perceval to form the next ministry, and harder for him to lead it.

Two letters from Mrs Thompson illustrate the times. "Your Father left yesterday to meet Mr Samuel Smith [one of Thompson's partners] in Lincolnshire", she told John in January 1810, "and we expect him no more till some of the wrangling is over in London. If that wrangling leads to immediate dissolution [of Parliament] he may return suddenly, but I suppose whatever events follow their investigations, some time will be taken for them to open out"[2]. Five days later she wrote again, surprised that her husband had got to London so soon. He had arrived there "frost bitten in the journey, and almost chocked [sic] with the sootiness of the atmosphere when he reached London. ... He

anticipates the struggle in the House which begins tonight. The Outs [sic] wish for enquiry, which is likely to lead to a new Ministry, and the K[ing] is said to determine on having a new Parliament. All this your Father says must not go beyond our own fire side, but as you have a legal claim to a nook in that circle, I suppose I do not err in whispering to you what you probably knew before. *I* shall not vote for a new Parliament, for I think it a very horrible thing; and it is a hundred to one whether they get a better". The debate of 23rd January, the first of the New Year, was a furious one, covering all the points at issue just mentioned[3].

From 1797 onwards the country had depended continuously on the paper currency described in a previous chapter. At the same time prices had risen steeply. From 1809 onwards, many people were claiming that the 'country banks' and the Bank of England had created the price rise by over-issuing bank notes. This, they said, had created "a quantity of money, and hence of money incomes, out of proportion to the quantity of goods available for purchase" (W.H.B. Court)[19], and had increased the price of gold. Thomas Thompson was a member of the House of Commons Committee on Bullion of 1810. That Committee judged that the Bank of England had issued notes more responsibly than some of the 'country banks'. It recommended a return to cash payments as soon as possible, and meanwhile a strict proportioning of note issues to gold reserves, as the only means of controlling inflation in prices and fluctuation in exchange. Whether Thompson himself voted for that recommendation is not recorded: it is not in line with his later thinking in Parliament. In any case, as Court puts it, "wisdom lay with the majority in Parliament" in 1810[19]. The Commons refused to accept the Committee's report, believing that to return to gold, even to escape inflation, was far too risky during a war in which gold might suddenly be needed to send abroad, or to meet panic withdrawals by bank customers at home. "The practical case for suspension [of cash payment] was that public spending must go on until the war was over; that suspension had become part of the system of war finance; and that the evils of inflation must be put up with in the interests of national security" (Court)[19].

While Britain fought France, each country blockaded the other. In 1811 Thomas Thompson wrote about the effects of the French blockade upon Hull trade. Merchants in flax, hemp and shipping had suffered, he said; and he described a flax and hemp merchant who had died, saying that although "the poor fellow" was not ruined, he had "lately sustained some heavy losses in the Russia trade, which drove him to dram-drinking, and most rapidly brought him to the grave"[7]. In the same month, Mrs Thompson and Philothea were seeking medical help at Bath. After "prowling about through wet and dirty streets" — it was February — they found good though small "accommodation" at No. 1, South Parade, Bath. Mrs Thompson arranged a rota for relatives to come and stay there; "except that I asked dear Thomas [her son] to come without specifying any time, because his health seems so important"[2]. Thomas had been back from Sierra Leone for eight months by then, but he had had serious fever when he left the colony, and it was still not known whether an official enquiry into his administration of Sierra Leone was to be held.

It seems, however, that Thomas had plans of his own, perhaps carried out more easily because his mother was away from home. In that month, February 1811, he and his true love, Nancy Barker, eloped from York to London, where they were married at St Andrew's, Holborn, on 4th March[6]. Johnson describes how Thomas gave the signal by throwing gravel at Nancy's window in Spen Lane, York, and how he led her to High Ousegate, where a post chaise collected them, leaving York through Micklegate Bar and carrying them on to London. Perhaps, as Johnson suggests, the bride's father and the bridegroom's father were too far separated in wealth to agree on the marriage. In the event Thomas Perronet Thompson made his own solution to that difficulty. His mother's brother, John Hobart Briggs, was a witness to the marriage[6] — as he had been, incidentally, to Mr & Mrs Thompson's in 1781[61].

Two months later Mrs Thompson wrote to John from another spa, Hotwells, near Bristol. One of the physicians there, Dr Carrick, had described its pretty riverside situation at Clifton, and its immense popularity at the end of the eighteenth century[85]. By the time Mrs Thompson went there in 1811, costs had escalated and the former crowds had departed[85]; but Dr Carrick was still there, and Mrs Thompson found him to be a "remarkably attentive, enquiring into every symptom, even to the minutest sensation ... He thinks Philothea in a tender and precarious state, though relieved at present from any very formidable complaint. He has ordered her a blister on the side. ... Your sister wishes to go out with me now", she adds, "[as then] the Blister will probably prevent her going out for a week"[2]. Poor Philothea, who had told John "I think, from all accounts, I should bear a great deal before I could submit to such a penance [as a blister]". The lamented Cambridge tutor Mr Sowerby had also been a patient of Dr Carrick at Hotwells, and had died there. He had not lived long after reaching Hotwells, said Mrs Thompson; "the whole internal surface of the throat, etc, as well as the lungs, was in such a state of inflammation". At the end of this letter Mrs Thompson wrote that she was "hoping for, if not expecting, an answer from your Brother and Sister to an invitation I sent them to spend a little time with us". As John's only sister was Philothea, the invitation must have been to Thomas and Nancy, married seven weeks before.

Johnson says that John, his brothers Charles and Thomas, and presumably Nancy, spent time together in London at this time[6]. John had his career and prospects in London, at Lincoln's Inn, (his chambers were at No. 21, Old Buildings, and the same building is still occupied by barristers today); but his mother seems to have worried. "Watch and pray", she wrote to him in June 1811; "I must say that whoever can ... in such a place as London ... spend their evenings in amusement and their late mornings in sleep ... and use no mortification or self-denial in the pleasures or pursuits ... must have learned an art which I cannot divine if they keep always within the bounds of propriety of conduct"[2]. (The words are similar to those which her own father had written "To my Dear Children" in 1772: "There is certainly a wide difference between those customs which may be observed with innocence, and those which injure the mind ... All excesses in eating, drinking and dress, all persons, places and things are to be shunned that tend to injure the soul. You can enjoy no tranquillity without innocence")[4]. Mrs Thompson wished that her sons would see their father, who was also in London. "He [their father] writes as though he was quite harassed and out of spirits. I earnestly wish you could see him, not for any very particular reason, but that you may give him pleasure, and cut off any cause to think his sons never visit him but when they want something for themselves. I believe you have met with invariable kindness [from him] of late years"[2].

Later that summer, she wrote that "we hear of T.P.T's arrival in Yorkshire. May we have a happy meeting": the meeting, presumably, referring to one with Thomas and Nancy. In the same letter she writes that Philothea was certainly not "proof against cold, or fatigue, or anxiety, either of which would probably soon finish her mortal course". Yet Philothea herself, now aged twenty, had written the month before, tongue in cheek, to ask John to write to his father about 'Cottingham Castle'. "Philothea", she quotes her father saying to her; "I intend to *run up* two or three rooms for us to use to live in next summer, and then the rest may be finished afterwards". Mr Howarth, whose house in Cottingham the Thompsons were renting, wanted it back the next summer; "so we are to *colonise* on the hill", Philothea went on. "But I pray you to imagine a solitary tower *run up*. I shall certainly venture, in some sunshiny hour, to propose a camp, such as the Gypsies form, as an emendation, but the tower should run down, instead of *up*!"[2]

CHAPTER 11

Wilberforce, Luddites and Lincoln's Inn
1811-1813

THOMAS THOMPSON WAS NOT WELL at that time. "Your Father has had some painful apprehensions ... and violent medicines have sometimes disordered and weakened him", his wife wrote in August 1811. "The medicines have been severe and sickening", she wrote in November, "but within the last week he has slept better, and though his appetite is whimsical, he does not loathe the sight of food ... If he avoid late sittings [in the Commons] he may perhaps be rather better than worse for his journey"[2]. It is recorded that he was absent from the Commons on sick leave in June 1812[79], but meanwhile, in March 1812, he made his first speech there since the debate on cotton weavers nearly four years before. (He claimed, in 1811 that Lord Carrington, in making him a Member, had "spoiled a very good banker and made a very bad M.P.")[79]. Now he proposed a Bill which would require Members who had become bankrupt, and who remained so for more than six months, to forfeit their seats. The Bill did not need much justification, he told the House. "A beggar should not be a Member"; and although, he conceded, there were honourable bankrupts, nine cases out of ten were due to "folly and imprudence". A country magistrate who owed money should not administer law from the Bench, he said, and Members should not legislate if they owed money. The first reading of his Bill was carried[3].

It was a better speech than his first, and the next month he spoke again, this time on the Gold Coin and Bank Note Amendment Bill. Mr Johnstone told the Commons that, because of depreciation, silver was worth less than before, and that therefore, when the State paid its creditors in paper notes purporting to be worth 20/- in silver, they were really only paying 16/-. In the same debate, fears were expressed that the £1 and £2 notes which the 'country banks' had been able to issue since 1797, might not really be redeemable for cash, as they were supposed to be. Thompson, as a 'country banker' himself, told the House that such banks now had £12 million of notes issued. Their bankers would certainly not *choose* to pay all that in cash, but their notes had been issued "in confidence of the solvency of the Bank of England"[3]. If the people trusted that solvency, he believed that all would be well. There is no doubt, however, that the war had brought huge problems to many people. That is indicated by the Bill passed in the same year "for the relief of insolvent debtors", as a result of which many debtors were released from prison[8].

"You have doubtless heard of the arrival of a little niece in York", wrote Mrs Thompson to John on 14th March 1812[2]. She added no further comment; partly, perhaps, because Thomas' and Nancy's first child, born at York on 9th March at the home of Nancy's parents, had been named Lucy Wycliffe Thompson. Both the baby's chosen names were from the Barker side — Lucy Wycliffe, in fact, being the maiden name of Nancy's mother, who was of the Wycliffe family of Gailes in North Yorkshire[92].

In September 1812, Wilberforce resigned his seat for Yorkshire on grounds of health, and took the seat of Bramber, which was not far geographically from Thomas Thompson's seat of Midhurst, and also a 'nomination borough'. Wilberforce said he had misgivings at taking such a seat, but decided that nobody was perfectly selected for Parliament[54]. Certainly his own days of usefulness in the Commons were not over.

In the previous month Wilberforce had written a letter, now in Hull University Library, to Charles William Thompson, saying that he greatly wished to heal "the breach in our family connections" caused by the Sierra Leone affair. He had not been able to do so sooner because of the possibility of a Parliamentary enquiry into Sierra Leone; but "now, I trust, this cannot be the case, and that I can be supposed only to be influenced by ... the general duty of Christian peace and love, strongly, I can sincerely declare, enforced in the present instance by my long and close friendship with your excellent father [Thomas Thompson], and by the recollection of the uniform kindness which from very childhood I have received at his hands". Later that week Charles replied, from John's address at Lincoln's Inn, that his brother Thomas was "activated by the same desire as yourself for a renewal of harmony". Apart from the fact that enquiries into the Sierra Leone governorship might recur, in which case his brother would have to testify "in defence of his own character and honour", Thomas wanted to assure Wilberforce of "the sincerity with which he received [Wilberforce's] friendly overture". Charles added that he himself was happy at the reconciliation, "chiefly on father's account, as the disagreement caused him most pain"[95].

There were many ongoing contacts between the Wilberforces and the Thompsons. Thomas Thompson, who was five years older than William Wilberforce, recorded in his 1814 memoirs that he had "owed much" to Wilberforce's grandfather, and had "endeavoured to show my gratitude to his descendants on every occasion"[1]. The ledgers of Smiths and Thompson's bank in Hull show various accounts in Wilberforce's name[63], though he was, presumably, not often in Hull. This book records some of the occasions when Thompson and Wilberforce fought the same causes in the Commons; and it includes friendly correspondence between Wilberforce and both John and Charles Thompson. Philothea, too, was within the Wilberforce circle, and seems to have visited them at their house in Kensington Gore (the Albert Hall now stands on its site) in 1818. "Mrs W. has been very kind to Philothea", wrote John in that year, "[and] Mr W. has all his usual brilliancy of imagination, applied always to important subjects"[2].

Meanwhile, in June of 1812, Mrs Thompson wrote to John describing the layout of the grounds of 'Cottingham Castle'; what she had called the 'policies' when in Scottish mood. Perhaps the soldierly arrangement of plants, already described by Philothea, made her feel the grounds were "not very tastefully laid out". Also, they provided no shade such as the family had enjoyed in the "long green walk" in Hallgate, Cottingham. The bedrooms, too, were smaller than the family were used to. "Yours [John's] is painted in a stone colour, with white Furniture". (Mrs Thompson wrote in the present tense, though it was not until June 1816 that the house was finally occupied). In the same letter she turns to a book, by a clergyman, describing the last days of John Bellingham, who had been hanged the month before for the murder of Spencer Perceval in the House of Commons. Bellingham's grievances were personal, not political, but at the time of the murder some had feared that his assault on the Prime Minister was a manifestation of Luddite terrorism. Perhaps Mrs Thompson shared that view, since she goes on "I wish all the miserable Luddites who are to be hanged, and all other criminals, had persons about them who would deal faithfully and rationally with them"[2]. The "Luddites to be hanged" probably refers to the seventeen who were eventually hanged in York on a single day in January 1813, as described by Edward Baines of the 'Leeds Mercury' — three for the murder of Horsfall near Huddersfield in April 1812, five for attacking a mill in the Spen Valley in the same month, and nine others for stealing arms or money[17,67].

That September of 1812 Charles William Thompson, Travelling Fellow of Queens' College Cambridge and officer of the Anglo-Sicilian Regiment of Foot, joined the 1st Battalion, 1st Guards, now the Grenadier Guards. Regimental records show that his commission was as 'Lieutenant/Captain'. The Battalion sailed from Portsmouth and landed in Spain that month. Charles Thompson appears on its roll a little later, which may indicate that he was already in Spain with the Anglo-Sicilian Regiment when he transferred to the Guards[32]. Alternatively, he may have done a short period of 'London duty' with the Guards, before joining the 1st/1st in Spain. One of John's grandsons wrote that John dined with Charles at the Bank of England "on several occasions" when Charles had marched his men from the Tower of London to mount guard at the Bank[5].

In May 1813 John, aged twenty eight, was admitted a barrister[38]. Legal registers show that he had chambers at Lincoln's Inn from 1817 to 1833[40], but his mother had addressed letters to him at Lincoln's Inn since 1811. Now, in August 1813, she wrote to him there to congratulate him on his "first appearance in the character of a counsellor", and to wish him "competence; friends; health; progressive virtue; and approving heaven". "Your old friends at York and Cottingham will rejoice to see you as a man of business", she adds[2]. It is possible that Philothea went to witness his first appearance as a barrister. (Mrs Opie was a great attender at law courts[42] although Mrs Thompson refused John's invitation to one when he was in York)[2]. "I hope you will not suffer from the heat, or Philothea either", his mother wrote; "but indeed she is too much of the Frog kind to be much in danger. Take care of her, for you will not have such another". In a later letter she joked about the law, and then withdrew the remark. "I hope that when you have 'tried, cast and condemned all the poor felon prisoners' in your circuit you will visit Hull", she wrote; but an asterisk leads to a postscript. "I am displeased with myself for mentioning this so lightly; and did it rest with you to decide causes [instead of presenting cases] I should enlarge on the god-like power of showing Mercy"[2].

She was right to say that the administration of justice was no matter for levity. No doubt John's work took him to the Old Bailey, from whence prisoners went to Newgate Gaol next door. Newgate Gaol had only been rebuilt in 1770, but it was dark, insanitary and grossly overcrowded. In 1813, debtors were there as well as felons, those with money paying for food and beds, the rest fighting for survival. In that year evidence was given of 340 persons in the debtors' section intended for 100, and of 120 persons in the female ward intended for 60. In 1810 there were fifty occupants of the condemned cells at one time, many of them waiting months for the Secretary of State's decision on their execution, and then hanged in batches of a dozen or more. From 1815, debtors were removed from Newgate to other prisons, which eased the overcrowding; but even so, when Elizabeth Fry began her work for women and children in Newgate in 1816, she was told that the female section was really too dangerous for her to enter[33].

Mrs Thompson's letters are not all solemnity. In 1813 she asked John, more whimsically, for a piece of legal advice. She was looking forward to news of her son Thomas; and at the same time had borrowed a library book. "We have got an expensive book of coloured Plates from the Library", she writes — "the costumes of Spain and Portugal. [One plate] has so strong a likeness of Thomas. Might not one in equity be allowed to appropriate a likeness that the public will not care a straw for, when it happens to be better than one can procure for money? On this principle, I should have robbed several works"[2]. Nearly two centuries later, have you not shared her conviction, when finding some gem in a library book, that nobody would really mind if you removed it?

CHAPTER 12

Hope for India; death in France
1813-1814

WILBERFORCE'S DIARY FOR 22ND MARCH 1813 reads: "Lord Castlereagh opened upon the East India Company's charter — [spoke for] three hours. Then Robert Thornton. Sparring about East India religious interests. I, [James] Stephen and Thomas Thompson [spoke]"[94].

The Company's charter was due for renewal, and there were religious as well as commercial interests to be expressed. Wilberforce's chief interest was in the former issue: Thompson spoke on both.

The debate was still continuing in June. In that month Castlereagh moved that trade with China, especially the trade in tea, should be exclusively conducted by the Company. Thompson, as a merchant, opposed restrictions which prevented British merchants from exporting their own goods in whatever ships they chose[3]. Two weeks later, when the debate was about monopoly in India by the Company, he told the House that "the people of the North Country could build ships to sail round the world as well as the East India Company". Captain Cook, he said, had sailed round the world in two ships built in Whitby. (Had he wished, he could have said that all four of the ships employed on Cook's three voyages round the world — 'Endeavour' in 1768, 'Resolution' and 'Adventure' in 1772, and 'Resolution' and 'Discovery' in 1776, — were built in Whitby, and that Cook himself had preferred their strength and capacity to more elegant "East India Company ships")[84]. Ships built on the Thames, Thompson went on, cost up to forty per cent more.

Furthermore, he said, it was ridiculous for the Company to claim a monopoly merely on grounds that they had had one for so long, and therefore assumed it would continue. The Company could not cope with all the potential trade with India, and thus, he asserted, British merchants should be allowed to do so before other nations moved in[3].

However, there was more to India and China than mere trade. Wilberforce, in the same series of debates, gave a most striking speech in favour of evangelising the people of India in ways which the East India Company had not previously permitted. Just as he had once told the House about the horrors of slave ships, he now described the horrible burning of Indian widows in the ceremony of suttee, urging the House not to call it a religious ritual which ought to be respected, but a disgusting festivity which Christians should seek to change. Thomas Thompson, in support, asked why missionaries should not break through the East India Company's restrictions and go into China too[3]. The result of the debates was that the renewed Charter of the East India Company contained clauses asserting that the Crown had sovereignty "in and over" the Company's possessions; that the British government should promote the "interest and happiness of the native inhabitants"; that it should expend a part of the Company's surplus net revenues on "the revival and encouragement of learning"; that an [Anglican] bishop and archdeacons should be appointed to India; and that

Charles William Thompson, in the uniform of the 1st Guards.
BY COURTESY OF MRS HELEN
THOMPSON-MCCAUSLAND

49

further missionary activity should be allowed. There was never a large number of Members present at these debates, and the Evangelical influence is clear in their outcome[53].

That autumn, 1813, the first of the Methodist missionary societies held its inaugural meeting in Leeds, and Thomas Thompson was in the chair[59]. No direct effort was made to raise money, though the idea of individual giving was promoted. It is recorded that Thompson concluded that meeting by "a ringing proclamation of loyalty to the King"; and "a paean of rejoicing" for the repeal of the Conventicle Act during the previous year, by which, he said, "the Methodists had been delivered from harassing perplexity"[59]. The Conventicle Act, a relic of Restoration legislation, had made it illegal for any person over the age of sixteen to attend an "assembly, conventicle or meeting", other than those of the Church of England, for purposes of worship[8].

The national Methodist Conference supported the Leeds missionary scheme, and thus the Wesleyan Missionary Society was formed. Thomas Thompson became its first lay Missionary Treasurer in 1817, serving until 1819[80]. It does seem that, after so many years of support for Methodism within the Church of England, he was now accepting its separate existence. He was still to be found supporting the best in either denomination, however. In the same year (1813) he spoke in the Commons debate on the Stipendiary Curates' Bill, denouncing the "crying evil" of clergy who held livings in one place and resided elsewhere, and urging that, at least, those who did the work in the parishes should be adequately paid. Forty years later Anthony Trollope was saying much the same thing.

On 27th November 1813 Mrs Thompson wrote to John, reflecting on the casualties of the long war. "I am sure you will join in gratitude that neither of your brothers' names are in the horrible long list. May all these commotions and slaughters lead to Peace!"[2]

It was nearly the end of the Peninsula Campaign. In the past six months Wellington had marched north-east across Spain, with many casualties from battle and even more from fever[32], and had crossed the border into France in October. Now the British troops confronted Soult's strong line of defence which ran eastwards from St Jean de Luz. Thomas was with the 14th Light Dragoons (Nancy was staying at her parents' and at her brother's houses near York). Charles was in another part of the line with the 1st Guards, a regiment which, his niece wrote years later, Mr & Mrs Thompson had hoped would stay in England because it was part of the Household troops[4]. It was rumoured that Napoleon himself was coming to beat the British. He did not do so, though an officer of the Guards said that every man in the army would welcome the fight if he did[32]. On 12th December Mrs Thompson wrote that she, her husband and Philothea had gone from Cottingham to Hull, "thereby escaping the bustle of Cottingham Fair, and being in residence to meet the missionary friends in Hull". Harry Green, a citizen of Hull, was proposing public fireworks to celebrate the British victories. But, "It is the Creator who gives victories", Mrs Thompson objected. "How wise we should look were half the Town to be set on fire!"[2]

On the day that she wrote those words, her son Charles was killed, shot through the heart and head while opposing an advance by French tirailleurs[6,32]. It was nine days before Thomas, in another part of the front, heard of his brother's death. "Alas, alas my brother. Alas, the man of my heart", he wrote to Nancy. "We shall sit together all night no more. I shall never hear his key in the lock again"[6]. The finality of it seems to have been too much for Thomas. The day after hearing of Charles' death he got soldiers to open the grave where his brother was buried with a fellow officer, Colonel Martin of the Guards. He took a little of Charles' hair, removed a small gold cross which Charles wore round his neck, and left a pencilled note in its place. "I think I have done to him just as he would have done to me", and told Nancy, "and I am content"[6].

The grave was in the orchard of Monsieur Commamalle, the local Mayor. Thomas recorded its position with precise compass bearings[6], and in due course a simple gravestone, inscribed in French[78], was placed upon it. Fifty three years after Charles' death, Thomas notified the Adjutant of the Grenadier Guards that his son — another Charles William Thompson — had gone to the exact spot recorded and had found the grave, carefully tended by the owner of the house[78]. In due course Queen Victoria, visiting Biarritz, heard that British officers were buried nearby, and sent a laurel wreath to the grave[5] — though no doubt it was just one of many graves in what had once been a battlefield. Later still, when the garden became a tennis court, Edward VII had a railing placed round the stone to protect it[5]. The grave can still be seen today.

Not long after Charles' death, his cousin Amelia Opie wrote a poem about the death of "my relation, Captain Charles William Thompson", which is printed in her book 'Lays for the Dead'. 'Weep not! he died as heroes die!', the poem began, in heroic style. It told of Charles' ambition to be a hero, of his great promise as a young man ('he might have taught and bless'd mankind'), and of his burial by 'toil-worn comrades' with no loving mother, sister, father or brother in attendance. The last stanzas of the poem reflect on the waste of it all; and later editions, printed when Mrs Opie had become a Quaker, turn the poem into a lament for war. 'Weep! *though* he died as heroes die!', these later copies say[52].

Wilberforce wrote in his diary (30th December 1813): "Saw in the paper, poor Chas Thompson, Capt in the Guards, killed. I shocked. Poor B. [his wife Barbara] turned to tears. Alas, Alas, I fear it will over do my good old friend"[94]. His 'good old friend', Thomas Thompson wrote in his own journal, sometime between February and May 1814, some pages 'On the death of my Son, Captain Charles William Thompson of the 1st Foot Guards'. "He had ardently studied the profession in which he was engaged", the father wrote, "with well founded expectation of rapid promotion in it. His character is drawn by Dr Milner, the Master of Queen's College, in a letter to his afflicted parents, in a way which was calculated, under the blessing of God, to give them much consolation". But the journal goes on: "Under this affliction I was less able to restrain my expressions of grief than on any similar occasion; and I felt that my heart had been more closely united to my Son than I had been sensible of. But I prayed for submission to God, knowing that all my blessings here are only entrusted to me for a short time. ... Perhaps I was becoming too worldly ... I had heard of the patience of Job, but, on trial, I found I had little of it". Other people, he told himself, had still greater losses. "In one day, without warning, God took away all Job's sons and daughters. In one day God took away one only of my sons"[1].

On 28th May 1814, at his hotel in Palace Yard, Westminster, he had the experience of so many whose next of kin have been killed in action. "I have just received from the Depot of the Guards, a large and heavy Box containing Books, Cloaths, etc, belonging to my late dear Son Charles, who fell at Bidart on the 12th Decr. last". He recalled a text from Ezekiel chapter 24: 'In the day when I take from them that whereupon they set their minds ... they shall know that I am the Lord'[1].

He does not mention that he and his wife shared the same sorrow, or even that they sought the same consolation together. No doubt they did, but his journal does not tell us so. Some of Mrs Thompson's own feelings are recorded in a letter which she wrote to John on 1st February 1814, six weeks after Charles' death. "In our mournful circumstances", she wrote, "I have found occupation a real relief. Though I by no means wish to banish the feelings of regret and tenderness, yet I have seen it a duty to resist the disposition to sink in sorrow. Might I have the supreme felicity of knowing that my dear remaining Children were girding up the loins of the mind ... it would be the greatest earthly comfort I could receive. I have been consoled by reflecting on the mercy of our heavenly Father, and his power to effect the preparation for that stroke he saw meet to inflict, and my hopes have overbalanced my fears as to our dear Charles' meetness for that kingdom into which nothing unholy can enter''[2]. What an awesome religion, which not only saw a son's death in battle as a "stroke inflicted by God", but admitted the possibility that God, even then, might not accept him.

An enlightening passage, which seems almost certainly to refer to the Thompson family, appears in the biography of Wilberforce which was written by his sons[94]. It describes Wilberforce spending the "Christmas holy days" with his family in 1813, and having his usual happy and relaxed time with his children. "I extremely wish to attend to them, but I sadly feel my incompetence to discharge the parental office", wrote Wilberforce at the time, in a letter which then goes on to say that he "saw in the newspapers that poor C.N. was killed. Alas! alas! I fear it will go hard with my good old friend his father. I used, I fear too sanguinely, to hope that God would hear the prayers of all who called on Him for their children. Yet surely good old N. prayed, and so did she, for poor Charles. Oh what a lesson to us all to give all diligence with our children as well as with ourselves, and also to live closely with Him, that our interest with Him may be greater! ... I have received by return of post a most Christian letter from my old friend. The degree in which the good man is filled with a sense of his own sins makes him dwell less on his son's situation, and for his own defilement the fountain stands open. S's [James Stephen's?] interesting account of poor C.N. — yet while eulogizing him, said he had no benevolence or kindly feelings. S. thinks that he was over-dosed with religion, and that of an offensive kind, while young. It is an awful instance, and well deserves the study of all parents; they should labour to render religion as congenial as possible. It is worth inquiring what the failure was in poor N's case, if any; which it seems difficult not to suppose, considering all his sons to be such as they are''[94]. The date of this passage, and its similarity to the words in Wilberforce's diary about "poor Chas Thompson" and about "my good old friend", make it almost certain that Wilberforce's description of 'C.N.', his parents and brothers, was of Charles Thompson and his family, lightly disguised under the surname 'N.'. It seems a harsh judgment, but an understandable one from the standpoint of Wilberforce's cheerful family; and "The sons being such as they are" was perhaps how Wilberforce did perceive Thomas, John and Charles at the time. It may only mean that none of them laid specific claim to Evangelical faith.

CHAPTER 13

Ambition, apprentices and dockyards
1814

ONE WOULD HAVE EXPECTED John Thompson to hurry home to give his parents his support after Charles' death, but two months later, apparently, he had not done so. His mother wrote on 16th February 1814 that she thought he would do so "when his spirits were equal to the interview". When he came, she said, he would at least find a warm bed. "Sibley [mentioned in various letters, and perhaps a bank clerk] has been sleeping in the Bank room near a month, to keep it aired, and help to wear away the smell of new feathers". She replied positively to an idea of John's about sending comforts to the troops near Bayonne, where Charles had been.

It was a hard winter in Hull too, she said, and she herself was "trying to do a little to mitigate the sorrows of such of the [soldiers'] wives as fall within my reach". Meanwhile she was anticipating "dear C.W.T's last letter" — whatever Charles had last written before he was killed — and was waiting anxiously for a letter from her "determinedly silent" son Thomas[2].

It may be that John, barrister of Lincoln's Inn, was not staying away from the painfulness of meeting his sorrowing parents, but because he had another subject on his mind. I do not know how he first broke the news to his parents that he had been offered a Professorship of Mathematics in India, under the East India Company, but we have a letter to him from his mother dated 25th February 1814, and one from his father dated the next day, from which it is clear that they had only just heard of the offer, and had reacted as might be expected

of parents who had lost a son in battle only two and a half months before. John's father was then sixty years old, his mother sixty one, his sister Philothea twenty two, and John himself twenty eight. Both parents had clearly discussed what they would write, as the arguments are very similar in each letter[2].

"Far be it from me, my John, to stand in the way of any apparent advantage merely on my own account", wrote Mrs Thompson; "but let us be satisfied that it is *Providence* that does it". "I dare say you will act as you have always done towards your parents", wrote Thomas Thompson, more bluntly; "and will by now have given up all thoughts of going to India. If you were determined to go, it would be such a shock to your Mother, following Charles's death, as would hurry her to her grave in a few months". "It does not appear that you would have an increase in comfort or respectability ... the chances are against it in point of health ... and the annuity of £250 is trifling", wrote Mrs Thompson. "The place is only fit for adventurers ... you may be carried off by the common disorders before twelve months out of twelve years ... and £250 is perfectly contemptible", said his father. (So it was to be for twelve years!). "The life of a man consists not in the abundance that he possesseth, though £2500 [the salary] sounds considerable", wrote John's mother. "It is too dear a rate to purchase worldly prosperity ... and you will be able to save very little of the £2500 per annum", wrote Thomas Thompson. "Your Father is very desirous of making you easy and comfortable", hinted Mrs Thompson. "I am willing to make you as independent as you can desire while I and your mother live", John's father confirmed; "and at our death you can probably have £800 to £1000 per annum". Then came the closing parental comments. "Nothing could reconcile me to parting from you", wrote John's mother, "unless you saw it a duty to go there to preach the everlasting Gospel ... but even here [in England], I should see equal scope for usefulness without the hazard". "I write with full conviction of the propriety of you refusing to go to India", said his father.

Thomas Thompson refers to 'India' in his letter; Mrs Thompson to the 'East Indies' in hers. Probably the post was at Calcutta, in East India. The question then arises why John Thompson was offered that post at all. There is no firm evidence, but there were several possible reasons at just that time. First, the East India Company's charter bill of 1813 had made specific provisions for a large sum of money to be applied to "the revival and improvement of literature, and the encouragement of the learned natives of India, and for the introduction or promotion of a knowledge of the sciences among the inhabitants of the British territories in India"[53]. John Thompson, as a Senior Optime — the degree next to Wrangler in the Cambridge mathematical tripos — was a capable mathematician. (It ran in the family: John's brother Thomas was a Wrangler, and Charles was a Senior Optime). Then, reference is made in Mrs Thompson's letters to 'Mr Dealtry', who sent the Thompson's news of Mr Sowerby's death, and was a friend of Charles[2]. A William Dealtry, Fellow at Cambridge when John was there, was Professor of Mathematics at the East India Company College at Haileybury from about 1806 until 1813[23,99], and although he never went to India himself, he may have put forward John as a candidate. Dealtry had become rector of Clapham in 1813[23], and was within the Evangelical world of Wilberforce, who may himself have thought that John Vincent Thompson would be good for India, just as he had earlier thought that Thomas Perronet Thompson would be good for Sierra Leone.

Whatever the reasons for his selection, John did not take the post. His father must sometimes have wondered whether he, as a promoter of foreign missions, should not have encouraged John to go. He half hinted at it by telling John of another lawyer who had gone out and had been reasonably successful; and by asking John whether he knew Thomas Middleton, who was to be the first Bishop of Calcutta. (Middleton was a hardworking London vicar who took a lawyer to India as his secretary[39], so John might have known them both). John's mother, too, must sometimes have wondered whether she had not encouraged John first to put his hand to the plough, and then to look back. Both parents, however, must have rejoiced that he stayed. Bishop Middleton died of fever after six years in India[39]. Thomas Coke, the first Methodist missionary there, died on the outward voyage[23]. John's brother Thomas sailed to India with his regiment and with Nancy that year, and was away nine years. John remained in England, a dependable pillar of his parents' later years — though his mother, even then, was not sure whether she could call him "an *avowed* disciple of the Crucified Redeemer"[2].

Soon after John had refused India, Mrs Thompson wrote that a Miss Harrison wished to send him a mourning ring, presumably in memory of Charles. She also asked John to look in his Chambers, at Lincoln's Inn, for a box of things she had once sent for Charles: "some stockings, and perhaps neck handkerchiefs, and books". "I make it over to you", she said; though the stockings she had sent for Charles on his travels would hardly be good enough, she thought, for a barrister to display beneath his breeches[2].

In the Commons, in May 1814, Thomas Thompson's first speech after Charles' death was in a debate about repealing the Apprentice Laws. Some Members supported apprenticeship because it was traditional; or because an apprentice received food, clothing and moral training from his master; or because the system of apprenticeship resulted in a trained work force which was not given to industrial action. Mr Hart Davis, however, cited 40,000 gun makers who would become unemployed when hostilities ended. Who would try to stop those men taking up another trade?, he asked. Thompson had already noted in his journal that "It is just to allow every man to employ his abilities in any honest way by which he may maintain himself and his family"[1]: so he told the House that he "liked liberty", and added a story about a town with two bakers, where "the bad baker, finding that the good baker had not served a regular apprenticeship, had him turned out, and got liberty to poison all his neighbours with bad bread". "Let those who choose it, bind their children as apprentices" he concluded; "but let not others be compelled to do the same"[3]. Those who think of Thompson as an entirely solemn man should read the reports of his speeches in Hansard. Each time he tells the House a pertinent anecdote one feels that the Hansard reporter, subjected to speeches all day long, enjoyed recording Thompson's.

In 1814 Thompson put a scheme into effect for giving land to the poor of Cottingham[1,28]. He persuaded the Cottingham church wardens to let some of the ground they had held, since the enclosure of common land in 1761, to the Overseers of the Poor. The Overseers, in turn, sub-let to families who had been receiving parish relief. The land was divided into twenty strips, each let for the very low rent of two shillings per annum, on condition that the holder claimed no more from the parish. Most holders built cottages on their strips. Many grew produce for sale, and did well; and the 'parish' was saved an estimated £200 per year. The last of what were then called the 'Paupers' Gardens', and which later times called the 'New Village', can still be seen[28].

Thompson wrote in his journal in May 1814: "I came up to attend this session of Parliament with some reluctance, and in a very indifferent state of health, and I am desirous of returning to Cottingham, my usual summer residence, as soon as possible". The House of Commons, he believed, could not do much about the Treaties of Peace — presumably that was the work of the Cabinet — "except in the Article with France relative to the Slave Trade". However, he added, he hoped that Parliament would give careful attention to the Madhouses Bill[1]. This was debated in June, when Wilberforce called for urgent consideration of the state of lunatic asylums. Thompson told the Commons that he had inspected several, and "had ocular demonstration of the abusive practices which prevailed in many of them. It was high time that those neglected places should be visited by proper inspectors. In York, particularly, great abuse was apparent"[3]. In due course a meeting was held at York, at which the Archbishop presided; and as a result the Steward, Apothecary and Matron were all replaced[1]. The Hull asylum, which had the active interest of Dr Alderson, was perhaps an exception to the general state of asylums at that time. Bedlam was not. "In Bethlem Hospital in London", Thompson had recently written, "Women are chained by the *leg* and by the *arm* to the wall, as has been stated to me in writing by some benevolent men, Quakers, who, with difficulty, obtained access to that Hospital"[1].

For most of the years that Thomas Thompson was a Member of Parliament he was also (1810-1818) Chairman of the Hull Docks Company. The portrait of him which illustrates this book shows him holding a map on which the New (Humber) Dock is specially indicated, and Cragg's plan of Hull Docks (1829) shows that the 'Old Lock and Basin', by which ships entered the Old Dock from the river Hull, was reconstructed in 1814 under his chairmanship[60].

He was much associated, in fact, with both Docks. The Old Dock, opened in 1778, had been a success from the start[36]. Built for less than the anticipated cost, it had soon paid large dividends to the holders of its 160 original shares; and from 1787 Thompson had controlled 23 of those shares on behalf of himself and his partners in the merchant house and bank. Almost as soon as the first ('Old') dock was built, it was clear that another would be needed. When that was agreed by Act of Parliament in 1802, Thompson was among those who ensured, eventually and after much dispute, that the new ('Humber') dock would indeed open off the river Humber, instead of causing further congestion by opening off the Old Dock[36]. It opened in 1809, the year before Thompson became Chairman. The cost of the new dock, with the much more elaborate entrance which the muddy Humber estuary required, was very high — but the Company, through negotiation, paid only a part of that cost. "I attended at my own expence at York the Trial between the Dock Company and the Corporations of the Mayor & Burgesses and [of] the Trinity House", wrote Thompson. "The question was whether, under the Humber Dock Act, the Dock Company could compel the two Corporations to pay one half of the expence of the Sheds, the Mud Engine, the floating Gate etc. Mr Rennie, the first Engineer in England, if not in Europe [John Rennie, 1761-1821], gave a most clear and decisive evidence in favour of the Dock Company; and his evidence seemed to determine the Judge (Le Blanc) in every point... My son J.V. Thompson was the Junior Counsel on behalf of the Dock Company"[1]. Thus the Dock Company was rapidly on a position to declare dividends from the 'New' as well as from the 'Old' Dock — despite, or perhaps because of the fact that the country was at war[36]. One copy of the portrait of Thompson holding a plan of the Docks is owned by descendants; the other has a prominent place in the Hull Docks Museum.

CHAPTER 14

Fit subjects for a journal
1814

THE LAST TWO CHAPTERS RECORDED events of 1814 which greatly involved the Thompson family — the news of Charles' death in France; John's opportunity to work in India; and Thomas Thompson's ongoing work in Parliament and in Hull. This chapter continues in 1814, and it records Thompson's sixtieth birthday; the celebrations of the first Peace of Paris; and the distressing trial of Thompson's brother in law.

On 5th April 1814 Thomas Thompson reached the age of sixty, and he began to keep a journal which, to a greater or less extent, he continued until 1827. It seemed to him that his sixtieth birthday, which came soon after his son's death, was a time to take stock; a time to begin to retire from business; and a time to prepare more consciously to meet his God. Keeping a journal helped him to do each of these things. It was also, as he mentioned more than once, a useful exercise in concentrating his mind.

There are places in the journal where, clearly, he went back and amended it. Sometimes he used the journal to give instructions, such as the notes to his will which he expected his family to act upon after his death. For the most part, however, the journal seems to have been an ongoing record for his personal use. It includes numerous religious observations and comments on the Scriptures, but these are always linked to his own active life, to events in his family, or to national events which were taking place as he wrote. It is possible that not all the journal has survived, but the four notebooks which exist, closely written but very legible, form a consecutive record.

The journal begins with a text from Deuteronomy which shows that Thompson did not consider life to be a random thing. 'Et recordaberis cuncti itineris per quod adduxit te Dominus Deus tuus quadraginta annis per desertum'[1]. 'And thou shalt call to mind all the way which the Lord thy God led thee for forty years in the wilderness'. Mr Little, the debtor schoolmaster who taught Thompson Latin, had given him a lasting gift.

The first part of the journal looks back to events of his early life, some of which have been quoted already; and to the recent death of his son Charles. 1814, however, was an exciting year, not least because of the abdication of Napoleon, his exile to Elba, and the preparations for the first Peace of Paris after so many years of war. Thompson observed those events, both as a Christian and a Member of Parliament. "Surely the nations of the earth will be convinced that the hand of God is in the successes of the Allies and the abdication of Napoleon", he wrote in May. "I have heard it observed [even] by profane men that only God could have effected such marvellous changes in so short a time". He relates how he was in London when Louis XVIII left England to return to France, and how "the good wishes of the whole [English] nation seemed to accompany him". He saw Nicholas, Emperor of Russia and Frederick William, King of Prussia received by the London crowd. "Wherever they go, multitudes of

I was born on the
5th April 1754 &
baptized on the
9th of the same month.
Vide, the Register
of my Baptism in
the Church of Swine
in Holderness.
Tho. Thompson

Reminiscences
at the
Age of sixty;
Anno Domini 1814.

Recordaberis cuncti itineris p
quod adduxit te Dominus Deu
tuus quadraginta annis per dese
Deuteron. Cap

First page of Thomas Thompson's journal (1814).

people flock to see them, and would often block up the streets if the Military was not employed to keep them open''. For himself, however, in the "quiet lodgings" of Henderson's Hotel, Palace Yard, "I have seen but little of the tumultuous rejoicings''. Not only was he "in indifferent health'', but he had recently received, in that same hotel, the box of Charles' property from the Guards Depot.

The Emperor of Russia and the King of Prussia both visited the House of Commons while they were in England. Thompson anticipated, in his journal, that "Members will not descend to any practice inconsistent with the ancient Rules and Dignity of the House''; and he was not disappointed. He was in the Side Gallery of the House some days later when both those monarchs spent some time in the same Gallery, listening first to a routine debate on distilleries, "which could not be very entertaining to them'', and then to a lively discussion of the proposed marriage of Princess Charlotte to the Prince of Orange; "which might tend to show to the Foreigners something of the liberties of Englishmen, and that there is no subject of which the House of Commons will not take cognizance''. During the visit, Thompson observed with satisfaction that — despite his own respect for rulers as God's potential instruments — "no Member who had his hat on, moved it, or took any more notice of these great Personages than he would of any other *strangers*, as persons are called who are not Members of this House''[1].

Two weeks later, at the end of the Parliamentary session, he left Henderson's Hotel for Hull, and "on Thursday morning July 7th, the day of rejoicing for the Peace, I reached my old habitation in the High Street, Hull''; and found the Bank quiet, despite the great confusion caused by the recent failure of Sheath & Co's bank of Boston, Lincolnshire.

The same victory celebrations in London had been observed by two ladies connected with the Thompson family. These were Amelia Opie and John Thompson's future wife, Margaret Alderson. The connections are shown on the genealogical table. Amelia Opie was a cousin of Mrs Thompson through the Briggs family. She was also first cousin of Margaret Alderson — though nearly thirty years older than Margaret — through the Alderson family. I have already referred to Mrs Thompson's somewhat disparaging description of Mrs Opie's novels: "her Girls seem invariably to *fall in love*''; but in due course Mrs Opie's book of poems, 'Lays for the Dead' contained tributes to Charles William Thompson, to Mrs Thompson and to Philothea, as well as to her uncle, Dr John Alderson.

Amelia Opie was the only child of Dr James Alderson, who occupied a similar respected position in Norwich to his brother Dr John Alderson's in Hull. She had pursued an active life in society, both in Norwich and London. She had married the Cornish portrait painter John Opie, who, like his contemporary Robert Burns, moved from a rustic background to a capital city, and impressed it greatly. Amelia Opie helped her husband into society, and when he died in 1807, at the age of forty six, he was buried in St Paul's. His wife remained, as a widow, in the centre of all that was going on in that early nineteenth century world in which social, literary, political, religious and scientific figures still seemed able to mix, and to discuss the whole of life together.

In later years Mrs Opie became a Quaker; never entirely solemn, yet willing to accept the disciplines of that life. In 1814, however, she had no such restrictions. She invited her sixteen year old cousin, Margaret Alderson, to come from Hull to visit her in London; and it coincided with the celebrations for the first Peace of Paris. According to one of Amelia Opie's biographers[42], the doctor's daughter from Hull, though elegant in later life, was found at that time to "eat nothing but pudding, tart and potatoes, and drank only water; and was often scandalised when her cousin [Mrs Opie] walked along the street, after a rout or supper-party, singing songs with her escorts, 'Lord This and Lord That' ''. Mrs Opie, however, was essentially a kind person, and delighted Margaret when she took her, "through meadows and market gardens'', to visit

59

Amelia Opie, in Quaker bonnet, aged 60. Medallion by David d'Angers (1829).

the actress Mrs Sarah Siddons at her country cottage in Paddington. The actress, then in her sixtieth year and recently retired from Drury Lane[23], was charming to them. "Margaret came home raving all the way", wrote Mrs Opie later, "saying that Mrs Siddons was the most beautiful, delightful, agreeable, and I believe even the *youngest* woman she ever saw; and she has put up in paper the bud of a rose which Mrs Siddons gave her, to keep for ever"[42].

Two other relatives in London, that summer of the peace celebrations, were Thomas Perronet Thompson and his wife Nancy. Thomas Perronet Thompson had returned from the war in France in June[6]. He and Nancy had stayed at Cottingham, and had then gone on to London. Thomas Perronet Thompson was in process of transferring from the 14th to the 17th Light Dragoons, who were serving in India. A letter to him from his mother[71] — the only one from Mrs Thompson to her eldest son which I have read — refers to an extension to his embarkation leave. This gave her son and Nancy an opportunity to return to Yorkshire, and she encouraged him to take it. "You will live at far less expence, and enjoy the society of the dear children [Lucy and Perronet], which I know will be more agreeable to Mrs Thompson [Nancy] than any attractions in London". She asked him to send what news he could, when he could. She and Philothea, she said, were less interested in "sights and sovereigns" than in "what sort of lodging you met with, etc etc". Long experience had taught her not to expect many letters from him; but "I hope I shall hear from you sometimes". She urged him to seize life's opportunities, and to "buy up the odds and ends of time" — which he generally did. She asked him, too, to "take all measures to keep up kindly intercourses" with his father: "so much of your comfort in life depends on standing well with him". That was literally true, since each of Thomas Perronet Thompson's Army commissions had to be purchased, and Thomas Thompson paid his son an annual allowance as well. However, Mrs Thompson's encouragement of "kindly intercourses" was not just to ensure her son's financial security. Evidently the coolness between son and father, which had existed since the 'young Governor's' work in Sierra Leone had been thwarted by the Evangelicals, still continued[6]. The same letter from Mrs Thompson refers to matters which still remained unsettled between the government and her son, four years after his return from Africa. Furthermore, it seems, Thomas Perronet Thompson's clash with the Evangelical 'establishment' had soured any orthodox Christian beliefs which he might have once had. "I hope you may light on some religious exercises agreeable to your enlightened judgment", writes his mother, not unsympathetically; though a simple faith, she was sure, was still the most important asset which he could acquire in life.

Three days after Mrs Thompson wrote this letter to her son, her husband was "at Barton Waterside, on my way first to Spalding, for a meeting about draining the Fens, and thence to Parliament in London"[1]. In this year, he said, another of his activities had been to promote Methodist preaching. The large new chapel at Waltham Street, Hull, was full: "The Methodists build chapels with great facility, while pious persons who are so attached to the Church of England as to do little out of it, find great difficulty in erecting Churches". The Cottingham Methodist Chapel, erected in 1811, was extensively altered that year, largely through his efforts[25], and perhaps to mark his sixtieth birthday.

It was not his only piece of building that year. "Late in this year, 1814", he wrote in November, "I began to build a dwelling House of moderate size, called by many, 'Cottingham Castle' ". The boundary walls and stables had been built in 1808, but he had "delayed to build a House in hopes that materials would be cheaper". Now, he estimated, it would cost £1800 to build the house; "but if I finish for £2100 I shall be satisfied". "I sometimes look forward with pleasing expectation that I may live in this House", he goes on, "but before it is finished, I may be carried to the grave. May I have a house not made with hands, eternal in the Heavens!"[1]

Cottingham Castle (completed 1816). Photograph taken before 1861, when the Castle was destroyed.

COPY BY COURTESY OF DR KENNETH GREEN

On 4th November 1814 Mrs Thompson wrote to John: "I suppose Thomas' prospect [in the Army] is India... Though I shall probably see him no more in this world, I shall be perfectly content if I have reason to hope for a joyful meeting in a better"[2]. Thomas was on his way East with a detachment of Dragoons[6]. Nancy went with him. They left their children, Lucy aged two and Perronet aged one in England with Nancy's parents, the Rev Thomas Barker and Mrs Lucy Barker, who had moved four or five miles, in 1813, from their parish in York to the riverside parish of Acaster Malbis[12].

At this time, sadly, a new concern was to come upon Thomas Thompson and his wife.

Thompson had two sisters, Jane and Anne. Jane, who was unmarried, often visited her brother's family, and often appears in their letters. Anne had married an attorney named Thomas Wainewright, and they seem to have lived at Wakefield[5], though Thomas Wainewright practised in Leeds, in partnership with one Joseph Blackburn[5,17]. There was one son, Thomas Thompson Wainewright, of whom Mrs Thompson wrote in 1813, when the youth was fifteen: "T.T. Wainewright [sic] is going tomorrow into Mr Sykes's Counting House ... I hope it will suit. He was to have come into the Bank, but the other turning up first is, I hope, providential; as I do not think that the sleeping in the Bank, among other things, would have suited"[2].

On 20th December 1814, Thomas Wainewright, attorney, was arrested in Leeds, along with Joseph Blackburn, and on Christmas Day they were committed to York Castle. The charge against Blackburn was of forging or counterfeiting revenue stamps on deeds and securities. If he was found guilty, the penalty was death. The charge against Wainewright was of removing stamps from existing deeds and transferring them to new ones, with intent to defraud the Revenue[17].

There is a detailed printed account of Blackburn's trial, in March 1815, written at the time[17], which also refers to his co-defendant Wainewright. The judge was Simon Le Blanc, who had tried the Luddites hanged at York in January 1813[23]. Blackburn's chief defence counsel was James Scarlett, later Lord Abinger, who had a reputation for not preparing his cases very carefully[23]. At all events, much was left to witnesses to Blackburn's good character, and that was not enough. Blackburn was condemned to death, and he was hanged at York on Saturday 8th April 1815, although a dramatic attempt was made by many of his friends to obtain the Prince Regent's mercy. In passing sentence of death, which in those days was done on the last day of the Assizes, with all those capitally convicted standing in the dock together, the judge singled out Blackburn as one who had betrayed his position of trust as a lawyer. As the prosecution had said during his trial, he had not just defrauded the Revenue; but, by removing stamps from people's deeds, he had endangered those persons' rights to their property as well[17].

Thomas Wainewright was charged, with Blackburn, on the lesser, non-capital offence of defrauding; and once Blackburn was convicted on the major charge of counterfeiting, both men were acquitted on the minor charge. Perhaps Wainewright was lucky. Certainly one family record states that he went by coach to attend Blackburn's hanging, and heard people on the coach say that the partner was as guilty as the man who had to die[5]. The point for us is the effect, on the eminently respectable Thompson family, of Thomas Thompson's brother-in-law being placed on trial at all.

Thompson makes absolutely no reference to the matter in his journal; but a descendant wrote that his sister, Anne Wainewright, left her husband because of it[5]. Two years later her son, Thomas Thompson Wainewright, died at the age of nineteen. There is a tablet to him in the north choir aisle of Beverley Minster, showing his address as Molescroft Cottage, Beverley. Molescroft Cottage stood on the site of the later White House, Molescroft. The cottage was built about 1816[83], and perhaps Thomas Thompson bought it for his sister and her son.

I know of no letters which express the family's undoubted shock at Wainewright's trial: but almost as significant, for me, is the family record that one day, perhaps forty years later, a man with a similar name to Thomas Thompson Wainewright was reported to be on trial at Leeds Assizes. Messages at once flew round the Thompson family asking whether this could be their kinsman, whose father had been tried at York for fraud, and had perhaps passed on a propensity for crime to his son: until the family was reminded that their kinsman had actually died at Beverley forty years before, whilst still a youth of nineteen[5].

The Eye of York. Showing the grass area where Thompson assisted Wilberforce's election (1806 and 1807); the Law Courts (right *where his son represented the Hull Docks Company (1809); and the Prison (centre) where his brother-in-law awaited trial, and where* *(left end of prison) Blackburn was hanged.* BY COURTESY OF ANDY WILLIAMS PHOTO LIBRARY, GUILDFORD

CHAPTER 15

Corn Laws, Waterloo, and a Workhouse
1815

ON 22ND FEBRUARY 1815 Thomas Thompson left Hull to attend Parliament, and reached London two days later. The important subject in this new session of Parliament, he noted in his journal, would be "regulating the importation of Foreign Corn, with a view to the protection of the growers of Corn in England, Scotland and Ireland"[1].

At that time the price of bread made from English grain was increasing everywhere, but cheaper corn was available from abroad now that Napoleon's 'continental system' no longer kept it out of the country. The Corn Bill sought to restrict the import of foreign corn, or to prevent it altogether. Thomas Thompson was in favour of the Bill, though there were many petitions against it. Mr Moore, for example, presenting the Commons with 9000 signatures from Coventry against it, told the House that his petitioners understood the difficulties of wartime, but that now it was almost peace again. Mr John Smith believed that the country could not grow enough grain for itself anyway, and was bound to import. Lord Milton, one of the Members for Yorkshire, declared himself undecided, because if imported corn was cheap, bread would indeed be cheap to buy; but it threw English labourers out of work because the farmers could not afford to pay them. Thomas Thompson, speaking on 3rd March, supported Lord Milton, saying that "In a small village near Hull, he inquired [sic] what was the reason for the distress of the labouring poor, now that corn was at

such a reduced price. 'Why, Sir', said one, 'it is very true that corn can be purchased cheaper; but this is of no importance to us, for we can get no work, and consequently have not the means of buying it'". When Thompson asked them why there was no work, they replied 'The farmers have no money, and cannot pay us for our labour'. "Mr Thompson", Hansard records, "did not want the farmers to have a very high price for their corn; but he wished them to have such a price as would protect them in their labours". A subsequent speaker accused Thompson of supporting the country farmers because he was a country banker; but cries of 'No, no!' were heard in the House[3].

The following week Thompson wrote in his journal that "the populace in London has taken alarm", regarding the Corn Bill, "and a Mob has filled the avenues to the House of Commons, and insulted several of the Members". The Speaker asked the Magistrates to protect Members. The Magistrates reported that their own Constables had done what they could, but had then had to call in "horse soldiers". Since part of Thompson's speech of 3rd September had been reported in the newspapers, he himself "did not expect to escape without some mark of popular vengeance"; but he walked the streets unharmed. He had heard that, in Hull, "my name is written on the walls accompanied with strong expressions of disapproval, but my Friends there do not expect that my House or Bank will be attacked"[1].

He expected the Bill to pass both Houses of Parliament with large majorities. Those Members who voted against it, he said, tended to represent the large cities, and voted to please their constituents there; and "the population in Cities, who know not how they are fed ... think of no effect which can arise from the Bill except an advance in the price of Bread". He asked himself whether, in fact, Members who tried to please constituents were "more at liberty to act according to the dictates of their consciences than those who represent rotten Boroughs, as they are called, without any restriction being imposed upon them?" On this occasion he had, he said, "voted in opposition to friends to whom I am indebted for my seat in Parliament, and I have been at perfect liberty to do so".

On March 17th 1815, however, whilst the Corn Bill was on its way through the Lords, public attention was briskly diverted elsewhere. "The alarming information has reached the Metropolis that Bonaparte has escaped from Elba, and has landed in France with about one thousand men", wrote Thompson. "Every mind seems agitated with the apprehension of all the miseries of renewed war in Europe". Over the next week various reports were received of Napoleon's march towards Paris; of Bourbon resistance; of Marshal Ney's defection to Napoleon; of British government stocks falling and rising with the rumours. "The Christian will ask, what is the end [purpose] of God in all these things?".

Despite the agitation, Parliament dispersed for the Easter recess. Thompson left the King's Arms Hotel, Palace Yard, on 23rd March and reached the Talbot at Peterborough that night. The next day he "went into the Fens by way of Spalding and Boston", and slept that night at Horncastle; "but the roads are very bad, and ought not to be travelled except in summer". The following day, "I easily reached Grimsby by way of Louth in time to save [catch] the Boat for Hull. I was thankful to God for ... bringing me to Hull and my Family again, and thankful for the spiritual privilege of worshipping God on Easter Sunday, 26th March, with

those who worship him in spirit and in truth". Unfortunately, the journey on deck, coming up the Humber, had given him a cold. "I became feverish, my head became heavy, and oppressed by a great collection of blood in the larger vessels, so that I apprehended all the serious effects of repletion of blood in the head. By Dr Alderson's advice I have been *cupped* in different parts of the neck three successive times (this is only a new way of bleeding), and I am certainly at this time greatly relieved. I have taken the Digit^S. Calom., James's Powder, and various other most powerful medicines, and I have sometimes in the last week concluded that my remaining days on earth would be very few"[1].

He wrote the above on Sunday 9th April 1815, when he had improved and was able to "sit, and lie upon a Sopha [sic], for a whole day". There is no mention in his journal, at any point, of the scandal surrounding his brother in law, Thomas Wainewright; but it does seem likely that his illness was made worse by the publicity which preceded the execution of Wainewright's partner Joseph Blackburn, at York on Saturday 8th April[17], and that it was a relief when that date had passed. On 13th April he was able to "go in a Chaise [from Hull] to Cottingham with my dear daughter, and on friday to attend a little to business in the Bank". He did not return to Parliament for the session from April to June, however: Dr Alderson supplied a medical certificate to the House[1].

In June came the news of Waterloo. Wellington's victory despatch was carried from the battlefield to the Prince Regent. The Prince read it with pride — and wept as he perused the long list of officers who had been killed. Thompson, still in Hull, wrote to Smiths Bank in London: "The successes of the Allies may be the cause of exultation for the nation, [but] the dreadful slaughter must be the cause of great lamentation to numerous families"[7]. "I have reason to say 'Bella! horrida bella'", he wrote in his journal. "It is now more than eighteen months since my dear Son Charles lost his life in Spain. My eldest son Thomas is now on his voyage to the East Indies [eastern India] where war is carrying on against one of the native powers, and it is probable that he may be engaged in it immediately on his arrival".

"There is now no doubt that Bonaparte has surrendered himself to the English, and that he is on board His Majesty's ship the 'Bellerephon', Captain Maitland, who will bring him to England", he wrote on 27th July. "How is this mighty, mischievous Man at length fallen!". A fortnight later, "Bonaparte has sailed for St Helena. He is treated with more mercy than he had reason to expect, after all his murders and multiplied atrocities". It was at a time when Thompson was active in publicising the Christian tracts of the Society for Promoting Christian Knowledge; of the British and Foreign Bible Society; and of Mrs Hannah More ("many of whose pamphlets are inimitable both as to sentiment and style"). He asked himself why, whilst the Allied armies were still in France, where liberty of conscience was now allowed, sound Protestant preaching could not be promoted there. He warmly commended "that wonderful Christian hero, Serjeant Wood, who fought at Waterloo ... and in the name of God cheered and led on his Company again and again to attack ... and is a preacher of the Gospel"[1]. In his writings, at the same time, he records the post-war economic confusion in England. "The distresses of the Farmers and Landowners in this part of the country are inconceivable", he wrote from Yorkshire to bankers in London in August, "and if the Country Bankers attempt to support them, they [the bankers] will be involved in the general ruin"[7]. Mowbray Hollingsworth's banks at Thirsk, Darlington, Durham and Berwick had failed in July: they had "pushed out Notes" without funds to back them. Now, in August 1815, Thompson's journal recorded that "farmers cannot sell several sorts of grain at any price; the price of livestock is declining; and a great London Corn House (S.G. & Partners) is reputed to be in danger of failure". It would be wise, said Thompson, if the government would help out corn dealers with loans[1].

That May (1815) he had spoken in a debate in the Commons on how soon the Bank of England could resume payments in cash. The debate brought various arguments about the price of gold, and about how the stock of Bank of England notes must be reduced in order to be replaced by gold. Thompson expressed firm confidence that the Directors of the Bank of England would resume payments in specie when that was warranted. After all, he said, if the Bank was suddenly to purchase bullion, the price of gold would rise, with an adverse effect on commerce and on manufactures. "For his own part, so little did he value a coin currency that if he possessed a thousand guineas tomorrow, he would carry them to the Bank [of England] and receive notes in their room, as being much more convenient"[3]. It was a boost for the Bank of England. Thompson did not feel himself obliged to praise that institution, however. Early the next year he assured the House that it need not think the Bank of England generous when that Bank lent the country money which the country had already deposited with it — and charged the country interest as well! "It put him in mind", he said, "of the negotiations between a Yorkshire lord and his steward, in which the steward agreed to advance £3000 of the master's own money by way of a loan — *and* to exact interest for it!"[3]

"In my quiet retreat at Cottingham," he wrote in August 1815, "I pray to be delivered from the anxieties and sorrows of the world"[1]. Yet ten days later his journal gives a detailed description of how he visited the Cottingham Workhouse without giving previous notice, "went into every chamber and garret in the House ... examined almost every bed ... tasted the bread ... and some fresh meat". The beds were clean — contrary to reports which he had received — and the food was satisfactory, but the thirty five children and fifteen adults staying there gave cause for concern. The children seemed generally healthy, but five or six were in rags, and the rest without sufficient warm clothing for winter. "The Mistress [of the Workhouse] says the Overseers [Overseers of the Poor in Cottingham] will not find Cloaths for the Children", wrote Thompson in his journal, adding a memorandum to himself, "Apply to the Magistrates if this be not done. T.T.''. Another "great neglect in the Overseers" was the lack of employment in the Workhouse, either for adults or children, and the fact that children were not taught to read there. In general, Thompson judged, the Overseers were sending large families to the Cottingham Workhouse when they could spend a much smaller sum on assisting them outside. It was no great kindness to bring them to a place where "the spirit of the parents is broken", and where both they and their children "sink into hopeless indigence and inactivity from which they seldom recover". Three days later he approached the Overseers, who promised to visit the Workhouse and "remove all just cause of complaint"[1].

In September, Thompson described the health of Philothea, then aged twenty four. "My dear daughter, who is growing in favour with God and her friends, has been for some time on a visit to [friends in] the West Riding, and I hope will soon return improved in health of body and with increased information of mind. I have no doubt of ... her desire to live and die in the favour of God. The state of her general health is not such as to justify the expectation of long life, but I pray God ... that she may not be exposed to great suffering before she reach eternal Glory". John had been visiting his parents and sister at Cottingham, "and we greatly enjoy his society"; but John's own health, his father feared, "is not sufficiently established to enable him to go through the labours of a Barrister"[1]. In fact, John had more than forty years more to live, during which he actively practised the law. Philothea had seven more years.

Apart from references in Mrs Thompson's letters, descriptions of Thomas Thompson's health come from his own journal. He recorded what happened to his body factually, not morbidly, and always with a sense that his health was within God's knowledge, and generally under God's direction. Life was not one's own; and therefore his intention to retire from business,

frequently expressed from 1814 onwards, was not in order to relax but in order to meet his Maker as he should. Perhaps inevitably, being the man he was, he continued both to work and to examine his condition until the end of his days. Thus in October 1815 he looks forward to moving into the new house at Cottingham — "not large, but pleasant, healthy and convenient" — early the next spring, and to having a Latin inscription, composed by his son John, carved there; but then adds a footnote that perhaps his mind is "too eagerly engaged in worldly things". "I have in former years been extensively concerned in Shipping", he wrote in the same month, "but in the beginning of this year [1815] I had left only a small share in a ship called the 'Pacific', and this ship was lost a few weeks ago on a voyage to the Baltic ... [but was] fully insured, and the owners will not suffer much loss". In that month, too, he observed the run on Moxon's bank in Hull. Customers tried to withdraw money which Moxon's did not possess; but Thompson saw to it that his young colleague at Smiths and Thompson's bank, Oswald Smith, hurried to London for a stock of notes in case of a run on Smiths & Thompson's; and he stayed in Hull himself, instead of in his rented house in Cottingham, until the crisis had passed. Then Mrs Thompson and Philothea joined him in Hull, where "dreary weather and painful coughs" could be faced more conveniently than in Cottingham. "I am thankful to God for an habitation in Hull in which I am settled with my Wife and Daughter for the winter", he wrote on 30th November 1815. "And this is a greater mercy as it brings us nearer to medical advice, which the health of each of us seems to require". He goes on to note that "In this old House in the High Street, the property of Mr Wilberforce, I have lived since the death of Mrs Wilberforce, his mother [died 1798]; but the expences of keeping two Houses may not be necessary when I retire from business"[1].

Two months later, despite further illness and thoughts of retirement, he was on his way back to Westminster.

CHAPTER 16

Lotteries, fisheries and factory children
1816

1816 WAS THE YEAR IN WHICH Thomas Thompson spoke most often in Parliament, contributing to eleven debates.

Leaving Hull on the morning of 6th February, "having been under the care of Dr Alderson for several weeks", he took three days instead of the usual two to reach the King's Arms Hotel, Palace Yard. "After having taken Garlick and various Gums prescribed by Dr Alderson for my deep and tearing and distressing Cough and Expectoration", he wrote, "I have taken copiously of Elix. Paragoric"; and he intended to continue with the latter "unless it should produce a degree of heavings or stupor in the head, which is frequently the effect of laudanum"[1].

"In my quiet and warm rooms in this Hotel", he went on, he hoped to be ready for business in a few days. In fact, further treatment by a London apothecary, Mr Seton, proved necessary. This involved "Ether, Squils [a preparation from sea-onions, recommended for the lungs] and diluting liquors". He did hear Dr Ryder, Bishop of Gloucester, preach at St Margaret's Westminster, however, and was delighted that there was at least one Evangelical on the bench of Bishops. The next month he met Dr Ryder at the Wilberforces' house. Thompson, at the request of Mrs Wilberforce ("that pious, zealous woman") told the Bishop instances of the awakening and conversion of several persons; and he spoke strongly of the need for a law to enable the Church of England to build new churches in populous towns, "where that could be done without injury to Patron or Incumbent"[1]. The 'Waterloo fund' of 1818, whereby the government voted £1 million for just such churches, was one result of such pressure.

Fine weather at the end of February made him record, in his journal, his wish to be "at Cottingham, preparing for my summer residence there"; but he decided to be "of more use to the country" by remaining at Westminster[1]. The month of March brought the Commons a number of strong petitions against the Property Tax, levied as a wartime measure but still continuing in peacetime. Thompson supported the farmers on whom it was imposed. This was a tax on profits, he said; and it was based on a false assumption that a farmer's profits were ¾ of the rent he paid his landlord. In fact, many farmers in recent years had made heavy losses, but had still been taxed on that fictitious figure of 75% of their rent. There had been more bankruptcies in Hull in the past ten months than in the preceding ten years, Thompson went on; and farmers had fared worse than merchants. "Like sheep, farmers have been shorn down to the skin", he told the Commons[3]. He added, in his journal, "I remember the state of the country during the American War, and at the conclusion of it, when England was obliged to admit the independence of America; but although the distresses of all sorts of people were then very great, they were far less than at present. We are now borne down with taxes, and a national debt unthought of at that time, and we have now competitors in commerce and manufacture which were then unknown"[1].

The alternative to a tax was a loan. A week after speaking on the Property Tax, Thompson argued strongly for that alternative. If the Property Tax was stopped, he told the Commons, country bankers could assist both farmers and tenants; but whilst farmers suffered that tax, everyone in agriculture would suffer. Some time before, he told the House, he had applied to the Secretary of State to have a poor woman and her children sent out to join her husband in Botany Bay, where the husband had been transported for a serious offence. This family had written to Thompson from Australia to say that "they now had their cows, and their pigs, and their poultry, and in fact possessed comforts which they never could hope to have enjoyed in England". Thompson told the House that he was now "assailed from all quarters by persons who said they understood he was commissioned to send out settlers to Botany Bay", and who in some cases asked if they could be transported (that is, asked if they could be treated as criminals in order to get there)[3].

He spoke, too, against the continuance of the state lottery, used during the war to raise funds. The lottery corrupted and endangered people's lives, he said; and a number of Members agreed[3]. The House returned to this subject the next year (1817), when Mr Lyttleton spoke strongly against the "dangerous, immoral and fraudulent practice of raising public money by lotteries"; the 'immorality' being demonstrated by the fact that the largest prizes were not paid in money but in government stock, and even that had to be used to purchase shares in a subsequent lottery! The Chancellor of the Exchequer then said he believed lotteries to be no more immoral than other games of chance — which caused William Wilberforce to ask why, if that was so, should the nation not obtain a similar revenue by "farming the public stews" (raising money from brothels). Mr Thompson told the House that "a very intelligent man" had informed him that during the sale of lottery tickets, "the bakers, the butchers and other tradesmen complained that they could get no money from the lower orders of people". There was no such thing as a fair lottery, he went on: "they were nothing but cheats and frauds upon the public; and the injury that the country suffered by their destroying the moral bounds and ties of society, was only known to those who were acquainted with the state of the poor"[3].

Soon after the 1816 lotteries debate, there were lengthy discussions of the government's 1816 estimates for paying the Navy. £43,000 was the sum proposed for paying the Navy that year. One Member proposed that the salary of the Treasurer of the Navy, Mr Rose, should be reduced from £4,000 to £2,000 (it was not his only source of income) in line with the government's pledge to economise. Thomas Thompson made a speech of high praise for Mr Rose's work in office, and urged him to take a voluntary reduction. "The example would be followed", said Thompson, "and the country would be satisfied that economy had reached the hearts and offices of ministers". There was applause, but Mr Rose turned the question neatly. He would have been most happy to take a reduction, he said; except that he had already done so on a previous occasion — and not a soul had followed his example!"[3]

In May 1816 there were further proposals, in the Commons, that the Bank of England should resume cash payments. Why not, it was asked, now that the war was over? Thomas Thompson stood up and expressed "confident hope that, in the course of the year, specie would be circulating in great abundance in the country", because of the great rise in exchange in the past few months. He hoped that soon "every man would have a guinea in his pocket", but he also reminded the Ministry to promote the "productive labour of the country". The wealth of the country, he said, lay in that more than in gold[3]. In fact, it was not until 1819 that Parliament agreed to return to gold; and it was restored to use in 1821.

Also in May, Thompson gave information to the Commons on the Greenland fisheries[3]. This trade was very relevant to his home town: Craggs' Plan of Hull, published in 1817, shows not only the 'ship yards' and 'timber yards' along the river Hull, but the extensive 'Greenland yards' on the east bank of that river, north of the town. Thompson refers to two aspects of the Greenland trade: oil and hides. He had already gone to the Board of Trade with fellow-Members of Parliament "J. Egginton, I.S. Bowden and S. Cooper" to request that duties be imposed on the import of foreign rape and foreign tallow, to encourage the use of whale oil brought in British ships[1]. Now he reported, in the Commons debate on the leather tax, that "fishermen in Greenland seas catch great numbers of sea horses. They bring home their oil and hides, and the hides are very thick and rough, like the bark of an oak tree. Many asses and bears are also brought from the North Sea". At that time 'sea horses' usually referred to walrus, and 'bears' to fur seal[93]. I have not identified the 'asses'.

The government did not do much for the Greenland fisheries, or much in general for farmers, although the Property Tax, the wartime Income Tax and the wartime Malt Tax were all abolished[1]. Thompson, for his part, wondered whether he was "too eagerly engaged in the discussion of political subjects"; but concluded that since he was placed in Parliament "in a Providential way, not of my choosing", he was right to contribute to debates. As he looked at His Majesty's Government, he found there "a reluctance or inability to act as circumstances require. They have not discernment to see *effects* in *causes*, or in any way to anticipate consequences". Furthermore, while reminding himself of the text, 'Thou shalt not speak evil of the Ruler of the People', Thompson could not ignore reports of the "most profligate" conduct of the Prince Regent. Mr Brougham had put it much more strongly than that in Parliament, and Thompson had found Brougham's speech "most violent and improper": nevertheless, if only a part of it was true, "morality and decency must hide their heads"[1].

By early April he felt his duty done in London until after the Easter recess. At the same time he calculated what it cost him to be a Member of Parliament. It had cost £100 for him and his servant to travel from Hull to London, and to live in London for two months. (He travelled by stage coach when he could, but as he now avoided travelling by night, he needed "chaises" for nearly half the way.). However, through the liberality of his "old friends, Lord Carrington and his Brothers", his seat in Parliament cost him nothing; so Membership of Parliament in fact, cost him his travelling and subsistence, "£200 to £300 per annum"[1].

On that April journey home he took the Peterborough coach from the Bell & Crown in Holborn (30 shillings inside for himself, 18 shillings outside for his servant). He was the only person inside. Outside were "three gentlemen on a tour of pleasure to Scotland, with books of geology, etc". From Peterborough he travelled by chaise to Barton on Humber, and across by ferry to Hull. "I return to my dear Family and Friends at Hull", he wrote "... and expect much happiness in their society"; although "a degree of disappointment attends all earthly enjoyment".

Returning to Parliament with some reluctance three weeks later, Thompson took the steam packet from Hull at 2 p.m. one Friday, and reached Gainsborough at 7 p.m., "the Packet having sailed about ten miles an hour. The voyage was extremely pleasant, and the vessel ... left behind every other vessel bound for the same place". From Gainsborough he proceeded to Retford, where he slept. On Saturday he caught the mail coach to Huntingdon, where he met two friends, and "we all diverted to the left, and spent the greater part of the Sunday at Cambridge", and heard good preaching. Thompson commented that there were evangelical clergy to be found at both Cambridge and Oxford, and that perhaps 2,000 clergy working within the 9,000 Church of England parishes were evangelical. On Monday afternoon he was in the Commons for a debate on the wool trade[1].

Back in Westminster he was soon occupied, with

Lord Lascelles (Member for Yorkshire), Mr Samuel Smith (Leicester), Mr Babington and "about 40 merchants and manufacturers", in promoting the merits of Holderness wool, and of Greenland oil landed at Hull, against imports from abroad. One Friday in May, he wrote[1] that he would like to escape "from this hurry of body and mind to the peaceful residence of my wife and daughter at Cottingham"; but the next day, Saturday, he was at a Commons committee on the treatment of children in cotton factories. That treatment, he noted, varied very much from place to place. Mr Butterworth brought evidence from some persons who did not wish to be identified, "as they dread the vengeance of their neighbours"; Thompson himself knew, on the other hand, of several flax factories in Yorkshire where the children were "treated with much kindness. The children are taught to read ... and as much as possible the sexes are separated, by which much evil is prevented". He was not happy, however, at reports from the mills of Lanark. "A Mr Owen, a wild theorist and supposed deist from Lanarck", he wrote in his journal, "pretends that he has effected a great reform among his 'operatives', as he calls them, by the system of morals and labour which he has adopted. It is said however that his people are very immoral, and that they purchase much more *whiskey* than formerly"[1]. Robert Owen had bought the controlling interest in his Lanark mill in 1814, and had recently opened schools there for children of all ages. He believed that the characters of both workers and children were formed by their circumstances rather than by any God, and that music and dancing might benefit a young child as much as learning to read[23]. Thompson, who wanted every child either to be taught about God or to read God's word in the Bible, could hardly approve of that. His journal of November 3rd, written after hearing a "plain and useful" sermon at Cottingham Church, addressed to 150 children of the Sunday School, and followed by a collection for Sunday School books, illustrates the point. "Teach children to read and think, and the way is open to the knowledge of the Scriptures, and the religion of Jesus Christ"[1].

Towards the end of May he returned to Hull via Cambridge, where he stayed with Dr Isaac Milner, Master of Queen's. Milner was having financial difficulties with an obstinate relation, and Thompson volunteered to write to the relative on Milner's behalf. He was glad to do so: "Dr Milner's constant kindness to my three sons [all of whom had been undergraduates at Queen's] demands my gratitude".

"Here I am on my way home", he writes in his journal at the George Inn, Grantham; in June; and the next night, at Gainsborough, "Here I am by the preservation of God, waiting for the sailing of the Steam Packet for Hull tomorrow morning at 8 o'clock". Since many coaches from London passed through Retford each evening, and many bound for London passed through Retford each morning, and Retford was only ten miles from Gainsborough, he reflected, travelling from London to Gainsborough by road, and from Gainsborough to Hull by boat, might often prove convenient to him. The next evening he was in Hull. "I am now here with my wife and daughter, to remain, I hope, to the end of the year [or to the end of the Commons' summer recess?] in peace and quiet. But I fear that the health of my dear daughter is not much improved, and that it may be necessary that she should remove to the South of England before the symptoms of consumption can be removed"[1].

Four days later he was at Cottingham, "making some preparations for the reception of my Family"[1]. The work on Cottingham Castle, nearly completed the previous autumn, must now have been done. Waterson says that the Castle, which was built of white brick with stone dressings, was "a rather monumental late Georgian two-storey, castellated building with a profusion of three-storey towers. The main (east) front had a large square projecting tower, buttressed at the corners, almost certainly housing the principal entrance. A dominant feature was the octagonal tower at the south east corner [the nearest tower as seen in the illustration], which was said to have been forty feet high". Waterson comments that the five towers shown in the illustration may indicate artistic licence[49]. Certainly the Thompsons spoke of the whole place as being rather too small, even for their quite limited family.

In his first entry in the journal under the address "Cottingham Castle", on 13th June 1816, Thompson remarked on the clear atmosphere there. The town of Cottingham was at a better elevation than Hull, and the Castle stood higher still, yet "below the frosts and winds of the high Yorkshire wolds". "I fear, however", he goes on, "that my dear daughter may not be able to partake much of the benefits of this retreat". Even during this long-awaited removal to the new home, it seemed prudent that Philothea should have the advice of "Mr Hey of Leeds, one of the most eminent surgeons in England"; and Mrs Thompson was to set off with Philothea the next day. "In two days they may be able to reach York, and in another day, Leeds". There were two William Heys in Leeds, father and son, and both were well known surgeons[23]. The son (William Hey, 1772-1844) may have been the one seen by the Thompsons, but if the father (William Hey, 1736-1819) was still practising, he would probably have been the elder Thompsons' choice. The father was indeed eminent as a surgeon in his day, and as one of the founders of Leeds Infirmary[23]; and the Thompsons would also know that he was a regular correspondent with Wilberforce on a range of useful concerns[94]. "Mr Hey", (whether father or son) had recommended Philothea to go to Ilkley for her health in 1808[2]. Now, though apparently optimistic about her, "Mr Hey" recommended an operation which, said Thompson, "Dr Alderson was afraid to attempt". Three weeks later, on 10th July, reports were good. "The operation seems to have been absolutely necessary, and has afforded great relief", wrote Thompson. "May her spared life be devoted to God"[1].

While Philothea and her mother were at Leeds, in fact, Thompson was under pressure from "the Methodist Preachers" — a collective term which appears quite often in his journal — "to return to Parliament immediately to answer the calumnies on Missionaries in the West Indies issued by some Members of Parliament (dealers in men) in the debate on Mr Wilberforce's Slave Register Bill"[1]. The clarification of who were and were not slaves was a logical step in the progress from the abolition of the slave trade to the abolition of slavery itself, but each such step aroused opposition, and this one did not have the support of the government either. However, the parliamentary session was nearly over, explained Thompson. Even if he hurried to London, he would not have the chance to speak; but he had written to Mr Barham, the Member who had made the allegations, for an explanation[1]. We today might add that his daughter's illness and his wife's isolation were reasons enough for not leaving home at that time. It was probably his genuine belief, however, that he should continue with whatever task 'Providence' set before him, because he trusted that his wife and daughter were under that same Providence already.

Still at Cottingham Castle, he reflected on the many bankruptcies in Hull brought about by speculation during and since the war; a number of them caused by sons bankrupting their fathers' businesses. "A confident, ambitious spirit will hazard all on the event of one adventure", he wrote. By contrast, "the prudent Christian merchant will show his moderation in contemplating prospects of gain, knowing the uncertainty of the issue of all human projects, and will not place in hazard so much of his property as may affect his reputation in the world, by rendering it doubtful whether he can do justly to his creditors by fulfilling his obligations to them"[1].

It was another month before Philothea came home to Cottingham. One day, during that time, Thompson reflected in his journal how Martin Luther had once spent three days and nights "on his bed, without meat, drink or sleep", striving to understand some words of St Paul. A fortnight later Thompson spent three dreadful days and nights on his own bed, "with a most violent fit of the Gravel, which produced inflammation and an immediate constipation or obstruction in the bowels. The pain was excruciating for three days and three nights, during which time I could only roll on the bed and on the floor, seeking for some position of body in which I might feel a momentary relaxation of the anguish. My medical attendants, Dr Alderson and Mr Watson, were extremely attentive and kind, and resolutely followed the only method of relief, most copious bleedings and injections, and it has pleased God to relieve me, and to raise me up, almost from the dead ... My daughter came home yesterday, for which I praise God, as her health is greatly restored. Thus my mercies are multiplied". His son John made an extended visit to Cottingham during this illness, giving up his attendance at Lancaster Assizes for the purpose. But Thompson himself was soon back at work in Hull, taking the place at the bank of "my young friend Mr Oswald Smith". Oswald Smith was usually in charge there — but was away through illness![1]

There is one more reference to his partners, the Smiths, in 1816. On September 18th Thompson crossed the Humber to meet Lord Carrington at Market Deeping. Carrington, the former Robert Smith, now residing with his family in Paris, had come over on business. "Many English Families have gone to France since the Peace", Thompson observes, "for the purpose of seeing the country, and of living at a less expence than in England. But to a pious Family, a residence among a people of such levity and irreligion must be particularly irksome and disgusting". It was with a sense of relief that he wrote, next day, having met his friend of forty years' standing, "I am glad to find that Lord C is not partial to French manners, and that he will probably not remain longer in Paris than next spring". Carrington was still active in business: "a large fortune has not made him indolent, nor has ability made him proud; and I hope that he may long live to be a blessing to his Family and his Friends"[1].

In October 1816 Thompson received a letter from William Wilberforce about the death of Wilberforce's sister Sally, who had been married first to Dr Clarke, a Hull clergyman, and then to James Stephen, one of the ardent workers against slavery. She was, wrote Thompson in his journal, "a woman of superior understanding and great vivacity, to which I have no doubt was in later years added real piety". Reflecting on Wilberforce himself, he goes on: "I believe that the divine renovation of his own mind, which was so powerful, so amiable, so holy in its consequences, tended very greatly to remove the prejudices which several branches of his Family entertained thirty years ago, against what they called 'Methodism' "[1]. He wrote similarly six months later, when he and Lord Carrington visited Wilberforce, who had been ill. "Few persons possess in a greater degree than [Mr Wilberforce] the conversational powers of pleasing and instructing; and these powers have often obtained for his sincere piety, a candid consideration, when it would otherwise have been condemned with contempt"[1]. When evangelicals seemed over-zealous, Wilberforce, who gladly claimed to be one of them, exhibited the charm and sympathy which were themselves an effective evangelism.

Stormy weather in November made Thompson abandon attempts to improve his grounds at Cottingham Castle, and seek "my more sheltered residence in Hull, where more convenience and comforts are to be enjoyed during the winter months than in the country". As he prepared to go, he read the 'Select Pieces' of John Bowdler, a barrister of Lincoln's Inn and contemporary of John Vincent Thompson. Bowdler had recently died at the age of thirty two[1], and his works had been published by his family. He is less well remembered than his uncle Thomas Bowdler, whose 'Family Shakespeare, with words and expressions omitted which cannot with propriety be read aloud in a family' (1818) inspired a new verb, 'to bowdlerise' — first used in print, incidentally by Thomas Perronet Thompson[23].

In Hull that November, Thomas Thompson joined several other Hull gentlemen "to consider what can be done for the poor". The Hull Poor Rate that year, he wrote, amounted to £16,000; twice as much as when he had been Governor of the Poor in 1800, which was itself a bad year. A calculation in his journal on 6th December 1816 shows that 9622 persons, one quarter of the total population of Hull and Sculcoates, were being assisted inside or outside the Workhouses. Efforts were being made to find employment for as many of these as possible. Meanwhile, charitable persons had given money so that coal could be purchased and sold cheaply to the poor, and so that good soup could be made and sold to them for "one penny per quart including a good biscuit", half its cost price. The chief cause of the poverty, Thompson believed, "although politicians of course are at variance in their opinions", was the cessation of demand for goods which had been manu-factured during the war, and the continuing burden of taxes raised "to pay the interest of the capital expended in the war". Others, however, faced a different sort of bankruptcy. Thompson visited a 'Mr B.', who "was once in great prosperity, and undoubtedly worth £50,000". But the imprudence of Mr B's sons had lost it all; whereupon "the father had borrowed various sums from *poor* people in order to support the credit of the sons ... but found himself utterly unable to pay the money which he had borrowed". Mr B's mind broke down, wrote Thompson; "and he is now a *maniac*!"[1]

CHAPTER 17

Habeas Corpus and Bridlington Quay
1817

ON NEW YEAR'S EVE, 31st December 1816, Thomas Thompson reflected that, since God had spared him thus far, "my conversation and employment ought to have a direct reference to a future life"[1]. For him, that did not mean retirement from present activity. On 1st February 1817 he was preparing to leave home again for Parliament, where the Administration, he said, could only hope to prosper if it undertook "the plans of retrenchment which the people expect and demand". Meanwhile, "the Prince Regent is unpopular, and is in danger of being treated very roughly by the populace". Before leaving Hull be presided, as Chairman, at the annual meeting of the Hull Docks Company, where a dividend of £50 per share was declared. It was the first dividend in five years, but the Company hoped now to give one annually. Outside in the street, during the meeting, several hundred people were demonstrating in favour of reform in the parliamentary representation of the country. From his hotel room in Palace Yard, two weeks later, he looked out on a meeting of 3000 citizens of Westminster, which was being addressed by Westminster's two outspoken Members, Sir Francis Burdett and Lord Cochrane. The speakers urged the crowd to oppose "defective representation of the people", all "sinecures and unmerited pensions" which wasted public money, and government waste of every sort. Afterwards the crowd dispersed quietly, as they had at Hull, and Thompson commented that Englishmen had more freedom to assemble and meet than any other nation, and made use of that freedom. During the next two weeks Parliament debated the suspension of the Habeas Corpus Act, Thompson urging that Habeas Corpus was too beneficial, in a free country, ever to be suspended for long[1].

No war, especially one as long as the Napoleonic war, is followed by peace at home. There is unemployment for men returning from overseas; unemployment for the forces at home (there were 12000-15000 troops stationed in Hull alone during most of the Napoleonic war); unemployment for those who worked in wartime industries and manufactures. By 1815 the industrial revolution had drawn whole families into factories, but had not yet given them security or proper working conditions. In agriculture, families were no more secure. Add to this the widespread famine which resulted from a series of bad harvests, and it is small wonder that, here and there, working men met together to think of remedies. The government was ill-equipped to deal with such situations. There was no national system of obtaining information on which to base its policies, or of assessing national needs in order to relieve them. Fearing the protests, and the half-formed political organisation of those who tried to make their voices heard, and the mob which might lurk behind those voices, the Tory government of the day reacted with repression. Habeas Corpus was suspended in 1817 after demonstrations at Spa Fields (Bermondsey) and elsewhere. It was restored, but apprehensively, before the march of the 'Blanketeers'. The yeomanry were employed to deal with the Peterloo meeting in 1819, and were congratulated by the Home Secretary on their action that day; and the Six Acts were passed to prevent all unauthorised assemblies.

At the time, perhaps, there was little more that the government could do if chaos was to be avoided. It took the 1820s, with their better harvests, higher employment, return to a regular cash currency, huge reform of criminal legislation, and introduction of policing, to make things appreciably better. Meanwhile, as the government's reaction to popular demonstrations hardened in the five years after Waterloo, many protested at it; and they were not all Radicals. Men like Thomas Thompson, who firmly believed that life should be orderly, could vote against the unconstitutional use of the military, (Thompson did so in May 1816), and for the restoration of Habeas Corpus (as he did in February 1817)[79].

The use of soldiers in Hull and Holderness during Thompson's lifetime merits more attention than it gets in this book. I have mentioned how the West Norfolk Militia — with its medical officer John Alderson — came to Hull in 1780 when foreign invasion threatened. I have quoted Jack Dykes on the use of Scots or Irish regular soldiers of the Greys or Inniskillings to check smuggling in East Yorkshire. Gillett & MacMahon describe a further military function; the use of the militia — always from another county, or at least from another part of Yorkshire — to control the Hull mob which regularly resisted the press gang or protested when food prices rose. Later, it was felt that regular troops as well as militia were necessary for this purpose; and thus, when the Scots Greys were sent from Hull to suppress Luddites near Huddersfield, they were at once replaced by cavalry from Sheffield, "it not being thought expedient to leave Hull without military"[54].

For those who held Government stocks, the situation was improving, and in March 1817, Thompson and his partners in London sold stock at a moderate profit. Money was "superabundant" in London, however, and the bank could not lend it out again at more than 4 or 4½ per cent[1]. That did not trouble Thompson, who did not seek high returns. He did believe in value for money, however, and shared the concern of his old Methodist friend Joseph Benson, whom he met at this time. Benson had doubts about the effectiveness of the missions in Africa. They seemed to be improving the lives of Africans rather than converting them. Thompson did not think that was value for money. "The Methodists cannot tax themselves merely for the purpose of *civilising* Idolators", he wrote. "The poor people of England who contribute their hard earned pence to the Missionary Fund expect more than this".

"By letters from my dear daughter Philothea", he wrote, "I have evidence that her mind is increasingly engaged in the service of God, and in labours of love to her friends". A week later, "I am longing for the day when I shall leave London on my return to Hull". (He planned to use the boat from Gainsborough to Hull again. On his journey southwards, in February, the axle of one of the boat's paddle wheels had broken; but, as he wrote, "the wheel on the opposite side continued to work, and with one wheel on one side, we reached Gainsbro'"). His health in the six weeks before this next journey had required the services of the apothecary, who had prescribed cupping for pain and giddiness. He left London by the Cambridge coach — "very fast, and preferred to every other carriage by the Clergy and other persons of the University" — from the White Horse, Fetter Lane. He travelled inside and his servant outside; and in the coach he talked with the Rev George King, son of a Hull merchant, "who remembered and reminded me that we had played together when very young at Hull". At Dr Milner's in Cambridge, that night, Thompson had sad memories of visits to Queen's College when Charles was there. Next day he reached Newark; the next day Gainsborough; and so on by steam boat to Hull. There he noticed the distresses of some of his neighbours "who formerly lived in credit and affluence". He thanked God for protecting him from "ruinous schemes", and decided to take on no new business ventures[1].

At Cottingham on Good Friday — he named the day in his journal, but made no religious observation about it — he wrote that he had been devising work for the unemployed poor. He was going to need 'chalk-stone' to drain the Castle grounds, and he would set men to dig it out from a hillside there. A man had a duty, he wrote, both to himself and to the needy. Neither duty should be neglected, but a rich man could afford to spend more time on the needy than a poor man could[1].

The next week he was at Hull Town Hall as foreman of the Grand Jury at the Quarter Sessions[1]. The grand jury ('grand' being the French rather than the English adjective) consisted of between twelve and twenty three 'good and lawful men of the county' whose task was to consider each indictment and to decide whether there was a case to be heard against the accused at the quarter sessions or assizes, where the 'petit' jury of twelve would decide guilt or innocence. "To find a bill, there must at least twelve of the grand jury agree", ran Blackstone's Commentary; "for so tender is the law of England of the lives of the subjects, that no man can be convicted at the suit of the king of any capital offence, unless by the unanimous voice of twenty four of his equals and neighbours; that is, by twelve at least of the grand jury, in the first place, assenting to the accusation; and afterwards, by the whole petit jury, of twelve more, finding him guilty upon his trial"[18]. It was serious work, and grand juries were intended to be kept incommunicado during their deliberations. That would be difficult to ensure in Hull, where the old Town Hall or Guild Hall in the Market Place had been demolished in 1806, and a new one was still awaited[19]. In 1817 a house in Lowgate served as Town Hall, with law courts behind the house. "I delivered a Presentation to the Magistrates regarding the Town Hall or Court", wrote Thompson, "stating the insufficiency of the Building, and especially of the inconvenience imposed upon the Grand Jury in passing to and from the Grand Jury Box. The whole is a despicable place, and a discredit to the Town. It is situate in the back Yard of a house in Lowgate"[1]. The magistrates replied that funds did yet permit a new Town Hall, and in fact it was not built for another fifty years[19].

In the same month as his grand jury service, Thompson drafted a petition which Hull shopkeepers might send to Parliament, requesting some relief from the ever-heavier burden of the Poor Rate. Meanwhile, he wrote, lack of employment was making large numbers emigrate from the East Riding to America[1].

He was back in London early in May, travelling "sometimes in Chaises and sometimes in the Mail Coaches, and sometimes *outside* the Coaches for the benefit of the air, and the pleasure of seeing the Country". His servant William Whitaker travelled with him, despite having received "a dreadful blow on the breast" from a falling lamp-weight in the house at Hull. At Westminster, Thompson was soon occupied with the Catholic Question: whether Roman Catholics should be admitted to the two Houses of Parliament, and to high offices of state. "It is said that national policy, and the perturbed state of Ireland, require it"; and Members were speaking of how "the tolerant and liberal spirit of the age" required it too. However, said Thompson, "it does not appear that the *Roman Catholics* have imbibed more liberal opinions from the liberality of the times. Their religious tenets are as exclusive, condemnatory, absurd and wicked as formerly". His journal quotes at length from the Papal Bull of 1816 which condemned translation of the Bible into the language of the people, and concludes: "I dare not vote for the measure [to admit Catholics to Parliament], as I see no change in Popery"[1].

Outside the House, he found himself constantly pressed for help by "various persons who come up from the country on parliamentary business", and he was urged by William Wilberforce to move for a Commons committee to enquire into the religious instruction of slaves in the West Indies. He would do what he could, he wrote, "but were I to sit in the Ho. of Com^s. till 2 or 3 o'clock in the morning, my health would soon be destroyed". Pondering the fact that God might, in fact, end his life at any time, he wrote a memorandum in his journal regarding his death. If he died at Hull or Cottingham, he wrote, he wished to be buried "in the Choir of the Church at Cottingham, without great expence or parade; and if my Children wish it, my name may be inscribed on a mural stone near that of my dear son Charles William, on the south side of the Choir". However, "if I die at one hundred miles distance from Cottingham, I have no desire to be brought from the place where I die". He also noted his wish that his sons Thomas and John, who would inherit the bulk of his estate, should, at the time of his death, pay all his servants, male and female, their wages for the remainder of that year and an extra year's wages besides[1].

In May he spoke in the Commons debate on Extents in Aid (for the recovery of debts owed to the government)[3]. At the end of that month it was possible for Members to leave Westminster with the permission of the House. Mr Butterworth, Member for Coventry, asked permission for Thompson to absent himself for three weeks on business. Apparently Members could not ask on their own behalf. Permission was granted to Thompson, but nearly lost on the technicality that he went into the House from the Smoking Room to ask the result of Mr Butterworth's request. "The Clerk, seeing me in the House, came to me and said that if I appeared there after leave of absence, the leave was void; so I made my exit as fast as possible!"[1]. His next speech recorded by Hansard was not until March 1818.

Spending Sunday in London before he set off for Yorkshire, he reflected that the Roman Catholics were at least right to promote "Spiritual Retreats" for prayer, self-examination, exhortation, and receiving the scaraments. He himself liked a Sunday of 'spiritual retreat' as an alternative to public worship, he said. He spent three nights on that journey home; at Stevenage; at the Angel in Grantham; and at Gainsborough. From there the steam boat, on that occasion, took eight hours "against wind and tide" to reach Hull. "By the blessing of God on my going out and on my coming in, I am now again at Hull with my wife and daughter ... to attend to business". The Bank, he was glad to report, had been ably run in his absence by Mr Oswald Smith, assisted by Mr James Henwood and other staff[1].

Philothea accompanied her father to the Dissenting Chapel [different, presumably, from the Methodist] at Cottingham, and together they inspected the boundary walls and gateway of the Castle, and ordered them to be built better. The rain made the Thompsons return to Hull. Wheat prices were rising, and insurrection in the West Riding made another suspension of Habeas Corpus likely. Thompson was considerably more disturbed by the rumour that "agents or spies of the *Government* have used various means to induce the poor people to enter into conspiracies against the Government, in order that the number of convictions may be increased. If this be true, no punishment which can be inflicted on those [Government] spies can be too severe"[1].

The weather became hot, and Thompson returned from Hull to supervise the workmen at Cottingham Castle, "and to enjoy the pure atmosphere of an elevated situation". He quoted, in his journal, the same poem with which his wife had commended 'virtue and heaven' to John in 1811:

'Retirement, rural quiet, friendship, books,
  Ease and alternate labour, useful life,
  Progressive virtue, and approving heaven'.
"I find far greater enjoyment in retirement than formerly", he admits.

His banking partner Samuel Smith, MP for Leicester, notified him that, "by a great majority", the House was not obliged to reconvene that summer, although there was much business to be done. The proponderance of rural members at the time is illustrated by Thompson's comment that the Government did not "deal fairly by the nation" in leaving so many matters to that time of year — June and July — when "country Gentlemen are obliged to leave Parliament to attend to their own affairs"[1].

At the beginning of July he was at Bridlington Quay, with Mrs Thompson and Philothea, taking the chair at missionary meetings at Bridlington (the old town, then separate from the Quay) and at Driffield. The meeting at Bridlington, held on a Friday, was "crowded to excess" to hear Mr Coultas, as missionary returned from the West Indies. Next day, Saturday, the Driffield meeting was crowded too. "I am much exhausted", confessed Thompson in his journal that evening, "and I must now recover my strength, that I may not be intirely [sic] useless in future!". The next day, "I thank God for this sabbath at Bridlington Quay". During it, he reflected on Deuteronomy chapter 32 verse 10: 'God found him in a desert land, and in the waste and howling wilderness'. "God found *me* in that desert land, Holderness", he recalled, picturing the coastal area between Bridlington and Hull. "It was a waste, howling wilderness, full of ignorance and sin. In this wilderness God led me about for the first ten years of my life, and then led me to Hull, where the light of the Gospel had begun to shine in a feeble manner, but where it soon afterwards shone gloriously. He has, I believe, instructed me ... and he has kept me in many difficulties and distresses to the present time. Ebenezer!"[1]. Ebenezer ('Hitherto hath the Lord helped us') was the name given by the prophet Samuel to a place where Philistines were defeated.

An early colleague in evangelism in Holderness, Mr R. Terry (already mentioned) had at a later date owned shares, with Thompson, in ships in the Baltic trade. Another shareholder in the same ships had been Mr John Robinson of Bridlington. John Robinson may have been son of Mr W. Robinson of Bridlington, "a most excellent man" whom Thompson visited during that missionary weekend. "I know few men who have laboured more zealously and more effectually than he has done for about sixty years for the propagation and support of real religion in the East Riding of Yorkshire", wrote Thompson, in a fine tribute. (Sixty years, if correct, would go back into Thompson's own childhood). "His house and purse were always open to pious persons ... and he was never ashamed to go forth with them ... into the highways and hedges, bearing the reproach of Christ. He has been the instrument of establishing the preaching of the Gospel in many towns within ten or fifteen miles of Bridlington Quay; and many times have I met him amongst people of great ignorance and rudeness, endeavouring to persuade them to forsake their sin, and to listen to them who came to shew them the way of salvation. He is now near ninety years old, and can do little more than pray for the prosperity of Zion, which is his chief joy"[1].

On the day after his proclamation of 'Ebenezer', Thompson had to call for a doctor, who treated his "great general weakness, and a pain and swimming in the head" with leeches to bleed his temples and a blister on the back of his neck. "Giddiness at short intervals, with nausea", made him return to Cottingham on Tuesday: he "hoped to attend to business in Hull in a day or two". Meanwhile, he reminded himself of a remedy which was surely gentler than bleeding, cupping and blistering. "In former years I was afflicted with pains in the head such as I now experience, and I was greatly relieved by wearing *fleecy hosiery* and strong shoes; and by promoting, in every possible way, warmth in the extremities". Dr Milner of Queen's College had recommended it to him twenty years before. So, "I must increase the thickness of my *stockings and socks*, and add woolen gaiters to cover all"[1].

Two days later, with or without fleecy hosiery, he learned that the Mayor of Hull was to sell the Methodists 360 square yards of ground in Mason Street, at 6 shillings per square yard, to build a Sunday School. Thompson promised £50 towards the building. (It would be well used: the Hull Methodists were already teaching eight hundred local children each Sunday). Later in the month he presided at a British and Foreign Bible Society meeting in the Subscription School Room, Salthouse Lane. The meeting, which was addressed by Church of England and Independent clergyman from London, was told of the good work of a Roman Catholic, Leander Van Ess, who was distributing Scriptures in the vernacular in Westphalia in opposition to the Papal Bull of 1816. The Society in London had already sent him money, and the "supporters of missions in Hull" now resolved to send him a letter of support. It was to be written in Latin, presumably because that medium could be understood in both countries; though in the end it was written in English, signed by Thompson and others, and sent off to be translated into either Latin or German. After the meeting, about seventy persons dined together at the Dog & Duck Tavern in Scale Lane. It was a "frugal and cheap dinner", says Thompson, but it gave much pleasure, and those who attended had "not only a feast of reason, but a flow of soul". He quotes the cost, 3/6d each, which hardly seems "frugal and cheap" when a quart of soup and a good biscuit cost 2 pence, but there were visitors from London present[1], and perhaps the cost included their meal.

Soon after that meeting Thompson wrote about "well educated young females in Hull, anxious to communicate instruction to the poor, and to lead them in the fear and love of God. Of my dear daughter, as well as of several individuals, young women of her acquaintance, it may be said, in the language of Cowper:
'With gentle yet prevailing force,
  Intent upon her destin'd course;
  Graceful and useful all she does,
  Blessing, and blest, where'er she goes'.
The modern reader may question whether Philothea's course was really 'destined'; but her parents thought that it was.

A few days later Philothea went to York with Mrs Thompson. John was to take Philothea from there to "Sir F.L. Wood", and then to come back with his mother to Cottingham. He and his mother brought the Thompsons' grandchildren, Lucy and Perronet, with them. Thomas Thompson described their upbringing in his journal. "For these two children, deprived of the care of their parents" — their parents were in India — "we feel great affection, and should be glad to retain them in our family, and bring them up in the nurture and admiration of the Lord. Under the care of their maternal Grandfather and Grandmother at York, it is

but justice, however, to say that their health is much attended to, and that they are better taught than they would be by strangers"[1]. When one considers that Thompson placed little importance on physical health, and much on other forms of development which he does not even suggest that the children received, his praise of the Rev Thomas Barker and Mrs Lucy Barker was less than enthusiastic.

He found himself, at that time, with "too many little anxieties about little things, and in much need of equanimity". One of the Emperor Charles V's generals, he reminded himself, asked the Emperor to dismiss him from the imperial service. When asked why, the general replied "Sir, every wise man would, at the latter end of his life, wish to have an interval between the fatigues of business and eternity".

On 27th August he noted that his son John had just left Hull for London, intending to visit Paris. It worried him. "I have great confidence in his correct moral conduct ... but where wickedness and infidelity abound, and where *Satan's seat* is, nothing less than the Grace of God ... can preserve a young man from acting contrary to the faith of the Gospel"[1]. By chance, another of Thompson's descendants has preserved a letter written by John to his mother on 1st September, describing the passport he had obtained for that same journey to France. "It requests all authorities civil and military who have anything to do with the Home Department of France", wrote John, "to let me pass freely to Dieppe. The passport contains the Arms of France, fairly emblazoned and signed by the Ambassador, sealed with the Seal of Legation, and signed by the Secretary of the Embassy; and all this for nothing. The only mode of identifying the Bearer is by his signature affixed to the Passport in the Ambassador's office. When I arrive at Dieppe I expect to receive a Passport in a different form, with the description of my nose and eyes, etc. I intend to go to Brighton tomorrow, and shall probably sail from there in the evening"[2].

A scribbled note from Wilberforce to John, written in December 1817, has also survived. "My dear Sir", it reads, "by a curious coincidence, just when the inclos'd was going off, in comes a poor Colour'd Washerwoman and tells me you are out of town. My Servant is spar'd a long and useless walk. But I will send ye letter as it is written, and when you return, let me know, that I may try to effect an Interview with you"[2]. Wilberforce, unlike the members of the Thompson family, still used an apostrophe for such words as 'inclos'd' and 'spar'd', and still wrote 'the' with the appearance of 'ye'. They were usages which were passing, just as fashions in clothing changed. "My grandfather", wrote one of John's own grandsons in later years, "well remembered the change in men's fashions from knee-breeches to trousers, and found the latter much more comfortable"[5]. That particular change of attire is shown very clearly by comparing Hickel's painting of the Commons of 1793, and Hayter's of 1833, both in the National Portrait Gallery.

As the autumn of 1817 drew on, Thompson wrote that he was dividing his time between banking in Hull and improving his property at Cottingham Castle. He felt he had spent too much time and money that year on improving the house; "but my Family complained from want of room", so three new bedrooms had been added, as well as a "Tower over the arched entrance". Now, he felt, they ought to be fully satisfied with the place, especially as — he added, rather lugubriously — "it will probably not be occupied by any of my Family after my death, and may be sold to the highest bidder"[1].

Reports from London were sad as well. "The melancholy news of the death of Princess Charlotte", wrote Thompson on 8th November, "has cast a gloom over all countenances ... The people of England supposed that a race of Kings might issue from the marriage of the Princess Charlotte, but now that expectation has perished"[1]. The people knew that Charlotte, daughter of the Prince Regent and his

heiress presumptive, had had a very unsettled life, but had recently entered into a genuinely happy marriage to Leopold of Saxe-Coburg. When she began a difficult childbirth she was treated with all the negative remedies of the times — no meat, no wine, constant bleeding and 'purging' — and she died. Not only that, but, as Thompson went on, the crown might now descend to one after another of the King's middle-aged sons, "and if all these die without legitimate issue, it may go to a Foreigner"[1]. That uncertainty did indeed continue until 1819, when the Duke of Kent had a legitimate daughter, the future Queen Victoria.

"The days are short and gloomy", wrote Thompson on 21st November; and the family moved back from Cottingham Castle to Hull for the winter. Thompson himself hoped to return to the Castle on two or three days a week for "field labours". He was there on his own on New Year's Eve when he wrote the following lines:

'I am alone at Cottingham this day for various purposes, but it ought to be my purpose to praise God for the mercies of another year which is now concluding.

'My servants are all at the Methodist Chapel for the purpose of ending the Year in prayer and praise to God, and I have engaged to sit and watch the House till their return, which will not be sooner than about one o'clock in the morning of the New Year.

'I am now within a few months of threescore years and four. It is not probable that I shall live to threescore years and ten ... and the decree may have gone forth. "In the year 1818, thou shalt die". I pray that in the New Year I may have resolution and strength to free myself from many incumbrances of business ... which press upon me with a weight before unknown". 'Non sum qualis eram' ('I am not what I used to be'), he had written in his journal that year.

CHAPTER 18

Forged notes and family news
1818

IN WISHING TO RETIRE FROM BUSINESS in 1818, Thomas Thompson had no fear, he said, of "*ennui*, or listlessness of vacant minds. I would not now leave unemployed the mind which God has given me, nor cease to think and speak and work for Him ... but it appears to me wiser to retire from the turbulent scenes of business[1].

In that year he made his last three speeches in the House of Commons. The first, on 17th March 1818, was in support of Savings Banks[3]. These banks were becoming increasingly popular; the Hull Savings Bank was just one of those established in that year[19]. In this debate, General Thornton suggested to the Commons that the rates of interest in Savings Banks should be kept low, in order to "keep out those for whom such banks were not intended". He then rather foolishly added that, in any case, "the lower orders" only wanted a safe place for their money, and were not concerned about high rates of interest. Thompson assured the House that the lower orders were much more sensible than that; but he did believe that Savings Banks should be for those of limited means, and he hoped that the more prosperous would continue to use country banks, or to invest in government stocks[3].

His penultimate speech, in April 1818, concerned the forgery of Bank of England notes. Sir James Mackintosh drew the attention of the Commons to an alarming increase in prosecutions by the Bank of England for such forgeries. In the twenty one years before 1797 — the year when cash payments were suspended — there were six prosecutions for forgery of notes, he said; in the twenty one years since 1797 there were eight hundred and fifty, and the rate was increasing. "What could cause this alarming and melancholy increase" in the crime of forgery, Sir James asked, except "the enormous and increasing circulation of Bank of England notes, especially small ones?" Thomas Thompson rose to assert that "the Bank of England notes were such that any bungling engraver could imitate", though a Bank of England committee had worked on the problem of forgery for fifteen years. "Country bankers had issued notes with impressions on both sides, and forgeries of these ... were very rare. [But] people in the country were afraid of a Bank of England note". A man had lately been hanged at York for uttering a forged 'country' bank note which he had bought at Birmingham. Thompson told the House that he had heard the man's confession, and although "he believed he had a tolerable knowledge of real or forged notes", he had had great difficulty in telling that note to be a forgery. By contrast, he said, the Bank of England notes were badly made, and the "roman candle figure" upon them made them still more easy to imitate[3].

A week later, on 1st May 1818, Thompson made his last speech in Parliament. It was on behalf of those who 'uttered' notes; that is to say, those who used them to pay for goods but did not necessarily know they were forgeries. Thirty forgeries of Bank of England notes

83

were detected every week at country banks, he said. The Bank of England suffered no loss by these forgeries, but the poor and ignorant, into whose hands the notes fell, might hang for it. It was "the peculiar duty" of the Bank of England to devise a plate which could not be imitated. "To what sanguinary persecutions must the present system give birth?", he asked, when one hundred and forty persons had been capitally convicted for it in the last year. Bank of England directors might "coolly, in their parlours", give orders to prosecute, but they ought to know and to feel that every such order was tantamount to an order for the death of a fellow creature; and that "the multiplication of these melancholy deaths was owing, in a great measure, to the bungling, clumsy manner in which their bank notes were at present constructed"[3]. The Member for Midhurst had proved, in the course of ten years in the Commons, thirty six reported speeches in the Chamber, and many other pieces of work as a Member, that his constituency and interests ranged far beyond the "one hundred and twenty blocks of granite" in the pocket borough which he represented.

"On the dissolution of Parliament in 1818 I was freed from all parliamentary duties", he wrote later, "and I sought not to be re-elected"[1]. Although the phrase may mean that he simply retired, there is some indication that he resisted an invitation to stand for Hull[79]. "I have seen much of the enormous expence and evil practices attending contested Elections ... At Hull [at the 1818 election] the contest was most severe. A Scrutiny was demanded, and went on for many days after the Poll had closed". In that contest between John Mitchell, James Graham and John Staniforth, Graham polled 1074 votes and Staniforth 1036[97]. In such circumstances men did not demand a simple re-count, but a scrutiny for malpractice. (Thompson's own son, Thomas Perronet Thompson, was similarly scrutinised when he gained a seat for Hull in 1835 by a mere 5 votes[28]). Thompson observed that Mitchell and Graham, who were eventually declared elected, would each have spent nearly £10,000 — "much too large a sum to pay for a Seat at any time, but especially during the present state of the King's health"[1].

He kept in touch with Parliament, hoping in that year that it would proceed to amend the Poor Law. The Poor Rate was reduced in many parts of the country in 1818, he said, because of increased employment, and because of the numbers emigrating to America. He believed that this was the time for Parliament to move towards "annihilating" the Poor Rate except in cases of extreme need: it was neither good for those who paid it nor for those who received it[1].

A letter preserved by one of John Vincent Thompson's daughters, Isabel Sidgwick, suggests that John was writing to his future wife, Margaret Alderson, at this time, although it was another seven years before they married. The letter begins "To my beloved Megginettina", possibly a derivative of the English name Margaret or the Italian Margherita. Written from Turin, it describes the contrast, as John crossed the Alps from Geneva, between "the men dressed in a sort of whitey brown flannel, with black hair thick on each side of their face, and a dingy cap like a sugar-loaf", and the inhabitants of Turin, "better dressed than in most English towns. The Officers of the Sardn. Court prance on fine chargers, and the clergy ... [are] more respectable than any of their townsmen". "I think it would be much better if you and Philothea had come with me to Italy", the letter goes on[4].

There was a close friendship between Margaret Alderson, who was twenty at that time, and Philothea, who was twenty six. Isabel Sidgwick, who was Margaret's daughter and Philothea's niece, described it in later years. Philothea led a restricted life, she said, but "had a few carefully selected friends, among them my mother [Margaret Alderson], who lived in the same town but in an entirely different atmosphere; brilliant, handsome, well dressed, and 'in society'; not much given to books, but accomplished and well taught". (The days of 'pudding, tart and potatoes' were apparently over). "The contrast between the two friends comes out prettily in some of my aunt's [Philothea's] letters. It is quite pleasant to find a petition [to Margaret] for the loan of 'the plainest dress Miss Clarke has made for you', that it might be copied 'to please my brother John' ". In return, Philothea promised a secure base to her friend. "You once called my room your ark" she wrote to Margaret Alderson. "Still think of it so, dear girl, and when you are weary of the world, let me take you in" [4].

A portrait of Margaret, with her first child, painted some ten years later, is shown in this book, but what did Philothea Thompson look like? "She was a good looking girl, with the strongly marked eyebrows of her family", wrote a great nephew in the 1940s, referring perhaps to some portrait which no longer exists [5]. "I once saw a picture of Lady Jane Grey, unlike any I ever saw, but very like your sister", wrote Philothea's mother in 1813 [2]. (It was possibly a picture of Lady Jane which she saw at Dalkeith during her Scottish tour of 1807) [71a]. Amelia Opie called her 'lovely' in the poem written after Philothea's death: "Pure, learned, lovely, gifted, pious, wise", was the description [52]. Philothea took a more light-hearted view. When someone once suggested she was "angelic" she brushed it off. "I have, on occasion, received the epithets of charming, bonny and blooming", she wrote to John when she was eighteen. "Nay, once I remember I was likened unto a *star*; but I have no *angelic* likeness" [2].

Mr and Mrs Thompson's grandchildren, Lucy and Perronet, appear in John's letters at this time. "Lucy is such a scribe that there is no competing with her", wrote John to his mother in July 1818; "and I understand that my Nephew is now grown much too fat to get into my pocket, which I am not sorry for, this hot weather". "I must buy Lucy's book to send with Perronet's Rocking Horse", he wrote the same year. Perhaps the rocking horse was not so different from a 'Chamber Horse' which Dr Alderson had ordered for Philothea some years before, in a different context. Philothea had been twenty years old then, and the 'horse' was to help her consumptive chest. "She seemed to set herself somewhat against it", her mother wrote then. "*I* mounted it, and thought the motion very pleasant" [2].

With the exception of certain journeys by boat, all Thomas Thompson's travels depended on horses. That year, he recalled an incident which took place in 1674. The Earl of Kildare fell from the saddle, and expected to be seriously injured. When he was not, Kildare ordered a sermon to be preached every year to commemorate how God had spared him. "Many times has *my* life been in danger from horses", Thompson reflected. "Once, when very young, I was struck by a horse and deprived of breath for a considerable time; and yet *I* have observed no anniversary thanksgiving for such deliverance" [1]. No doubt he knew the epitaph by Camden:

'Betwixt the stirrup and the ground
  Mercy I asked, mercy I found'.

The man in Camden's epitaph was killed by his fall. Kildare and Thompson escaped serious hurt. To all three of them, God was merciful.

CHAPTER 19

The Arab coast and the Yorkshire coast
1819-1821

IN 1819 THOMAS PERRONET THOMPSON, serving in India with the 17th Light Dragoons since 1815 and longing for change, accompanied Sir William Grant Keir in a major expedition against the Wahabee tribe. His wife Nancy accompanied him[6]. The Wahabees were Arabs of the 'Pirate Coast' between Abu Dhabi and the Strait of Hormuz. They were in the habit of plundering ships sailing through the Persian Gulf on the "direct" route from Britain to India which crossed overland from Aleppo (now in Syria) to Basra (Iraq) and continued by sea to Bombay[48].

Captain Thompson admired the way in which Keir dealt reasonably with the Wahabees once they were defeated. He himself, as Arabic interpreter to the expedition, took great satisfaction in drawing up a treaty between the British and the Wahabees. The treaty included a clause stating that in future, any carrying off by the Arabs of slaves from Africa, or any transporting of them from Africa by sea, would be deemed an act of plunder and piracy. It was the first such international declaration of slavery as piracy, predating one for which the United States claimed first place. The English language copies of this treaty are in Nancy Thompson's handwriting. Her work as 'political secretary' on this occasion established the place at her husband's side which she and their son Charles, born in India, tried to maintain throughout their Eastern travels[6].

The close contact which Captain Thompson had had with the Arabs led to his appointment as political agent, and garrison commander of Ras al Khaima, when Keir's main force returned to Bombay. Subsequently, as officer commanding a force of largely Indian troops against an Arab attack, he was severely defeated in November 1820; a loss for which he was court-martialled in India. The event, the trial, and Thomas Perronet Thompson's almost total acquittal are described in detail by Moyse-Bartlett[48]. It was an occasion of major interest in Bombay, and of lasting pain to Thomas Perronet Thompson[6], though his subsequent promotions show that his career survived it.

Meanwhile, John Vincent Thompson described a Yorkshire scene in a letter to his mother written from 'Mrs Tatham's Lodgings, Scarborough' in October 1819. John had his niece and nephew, Lucy and Perronet, with him. "Lucy and Perronet are greatly delighted with their Grandmama's letter", he wrote. "It is so long since I have been at any Sea Bathing Place at which I bathed", he went on, "that all the accompaniments of one seem almost new to me. The most common difficulty is how to get shoes or boots that will keep the feet dry in walking on the sands, and I have often thought what trouble you must have had in former days in keeping us all in decent stockings and petticoats"[2]. Ainsworth's 'Scarborough Guide' of 1818 and 1820 describes how lodgings might be obtained at that time, and quotes the usual tariff: "Half a guinea or twelve shillings for a room per week, servants' rooms at half price; the kitchen, with all utensils both for

86

cooking and the table, one guinea per week; servants' hall, half a guinea; the cook expects half a guinea per week". Boarding houses which provided meals for their lodgers are listed in the 'Guide', but Mrs Tatham's is not among them[9].

In this letter from Scarborough, John asked his mother to ensure that some shirts being made for him were large enough. It would be easier, he confessed, "if my face was more of the mould of Don Quixote", but, as it as, "... I should be glad if you would make the *necks wider*. The breadth of the Ruffle is quite correct". He then moves on to wider topics. "Sir William Strickland and Mr Dangerfield, who have been collecting those Snake stones [ammonites] which are found in this neighbourhood and at Whitby, discovered some time ago a whole fossil Crocodile on the rocks which are washed by the sea". They had waited for the spring tides to bring low water before removing the fossil from its bed, but in the meantime "some person from Pontefract" had managed to remove the back bone, with the result that the sea broke up all the rest. This was not the only such discovery: a fossil crocodile, *teleosaurus chapmani*, recovered near Whitby in 1824, can be seen today in Whitby Museum[93]. "It is supposed", continued John in 1819, "that crocodiles as well as elephants, a fossil tusk of which was found at Bridlington, were inhabitants of this country before the deluge. But as Providence always adapts an animal's habits to the climate and country in which it is placed, it seems hardly probable that those creatures which are now indigenous in Africa should ever have accommodated themselves to British soil"[2]. His argument was not quite logical. If Providence could adapt an animal's habits, it could presumably have adapted crocodiles to Britain, however different Britain seemed from Africa. That would be the fundamentalist Captain Fitzroy's contention on the 'Beagle' in the 1830s, when Darwin was discovering that, on the contrary, creatures adapted themselves to environments[46].

Early in 1821 John wrote the last letter to his mother which I have seen. He was at Lincoln's Inn, she at 'Bank, Hull'. Writing of relatives who had moved from London to Croydon, he says that, of course, "if people get rich and live in country-houses [sic] at a distance from their poor relatives, they must be content to take the absence of their friends as a tax upon their improved comforts"[2]. The remark may refer to the isolation which, to some extent, attended the Thompsons' move to Cottingham Castle; although the same would apply to any acquaintances in Hull or London who were moving out of town.

It may be that John, now aged thirty four, was under some pressure to be married, and even to occupy Cottingham Castle one day if his brother Thomas continued to travel with the Army. The same letter to his mother goes on: "I hear a great deal from Mrs Howden, and particularly of a *Wraith* of Philothea's who accompanies her, whose name I do not recollect, but everyone affirms that this young lady is the image of my Sister, a circumstance which does not give me as great a desire to see her as my relatives seem to think I ought to have. They do not know the original as well as I do"[2]. The remark is brotherly leg-pulling, and the 'Wraith' or image of Philothea remains unidentified.

George III had died in 1820, after a reign of sixty years which had almost spanned the lifetime of Thomas Thompson and his wife. The summer of 1821 must have made many reflect upon the nature of monarchy. Napoleon died on St Helena in May. Two months later the former Prince Regent was crowned George IV. It does not seem likely that the Thompson family would have approved of that squalid coronation, at which the king's rejected wife, whose daughter was not long dead, appeared at the door of Westminster Abbey — Amelia Opie was among those who witnessed it[42] — and was turned away. Nor surely, for all the talk of the inadequacies of the queen, could they have approved when the king virtually ignored her death. The London mob which gave the queen a funeral procession, if only to mock the king, had some truth on their side. I would like to have heard Mr & Mrs Thompson's views on the matter.

In that year, 1821, Thomas Thompson published his 'Ocellum Promontorium: or short Observations of the Ancient State of Holderness, with Historic Facts relative to the Sea Port and Market Town of Ravenspurne in Holderness'. In this book, Thompson assembles and quotes many records of Holderness in ancient and mediaeval times. 'Ocellum Promontorium' was the Roman name for Spurn Head recorded by Ptolemy. Thompson — still quoted as an authority on Spurn Head by Thomas Sheppard in his 'Lost Towns of the Yorkshire Coast', published in 1912 — placed the original Spurn Head on high ground, east of Kilnsea, which was washed into the sea at the end of the eighteenth century[73,75]. A number of villages all along the Holderness coast have been washed away since Roman days, and a particular mystery still surrounds the once flourishing, now vanished town of Ravenspurne, which stood on Spurn Point, the shifting neck of land between the Humber and the North Sea. Thompson expressed that mystery in the preface to his book. " 'Jam seges est ubi Troia fuit' ['Now there are sown fields where Troy stood'] was said of Troy; but the patient Antiquary, in his Travels in Holderness, may sit on the banks of the Humber and watch the ebbing of the tide, without being able to discern a blade of grass [let alone a field] where once stood the market-town and sea-port of Ravenspurne''. The name of the author, native of Holderness, is appended to the preface: 'Tho. Thompson. Cottingham Castle, 1821'[73].

From December 1821 onwards, Thompson used part of his journal to make observations on natural phenomena, particularly in the area of the Castle. He makes frequent reference to the rise and fall of water in Keldgate Springs, on the north side of his land there; and to the state of his sheep and cattle on that land[1]. In December 1821, for example, he watched the water rise, wondering if it would flood his carrot fields. It did not, and the next month his sheep were being fed carrots, which saved him purchasing turnips. He employed a man and a woman to slice carrots until he obtained a machine called 'Gardner's Turnip Cutter' from Banbury. The machine worked "with great ease and rapidity", and in February "the sheep now like carrots so well that if too large a quantity were given to them at once, they would eat till they *burst*"[1].

CHAPTER 20

"The dear departed Saints"
1823

WINTER WAS A TIME OF PAIN and difficult breathing for Mrs Thompson and Philothea. In December 1822 they set out in search of some relief, this time to Cornwall. Johnson's phrase is that Mrs Thompson took Philothea to Penzance "in the hope that the change of climate would arrest the consumption which was destroying her"[37]. Philothea's niece wrote, many years earlier than Johnson, that "There was always the strongest bond of admiration and affection between my Aunt Philothea and her mother, and when the mother's health gave way, the two left home together to try what Cornish air would do"[4]. Both women — Mrs Thompson was sixty nine, Philothea thirty two — were gravely ill. A family record says that they were helped, in Cornwall, by another Methodist banking family, the Carnes of Penzance, who have graves at Gulval[69]. It seems likely that the help came specifically from William Carne (1754-1836), head of Batten, Carne & Carne's bank[23], a former friend of John Wesley[91], whose wife Anna had very recently died[23].

Thomas Thompson remained in Hull, and recorded the beginning of 1823 in his journal. "On this first sabbath day in the new year", he wrote on 5th January, "my retrospect of mercies in the past year excites my greatest gratitude and praise". Nevertheless, that day he had had a repetition of his own previous symptoms — "fullness of blood, and pain and giddiness in the head, which have produced partial loss of sight". Dr Alderson had ordered an aperient, a "low diet", and

24 ounces of blood to be removed from the arm immediately. "It appears that the vessels have been overloaded and dangerously distended". Further bleeding was carried out the next day, with some difficulty. The danger was considered to be "an attack of an apoplectic or paralytic kind which, it seems to be the established opinion, nothing but copious bleeding could prevent". In the absence of Thompson's wife and daughter, his "kind sister Jane" had come from Beverley to be with him[1].

On Sunday 26th January he noted that he felt much stronger, although "by the loss of blood I am left very sensitive, and liable to be agitated by trifles light as air". "The mind is often harassed when the body is weak", he observed, and therefore he believed it right to "mix medicines with faith and prayer".

On that day medicine, faith and prayer were needed in Cornwall too. Thompson's journal goes on: "A new and sudden affliction is about to come upon me. My daughter writes from Penzance that her dear Mother had a slight apoplectic fit on sunday night the 26th January, but that on monday morning she was much better; and this report of amendment was confirmed by Mr Giddy, the medical attendant. But still from various increasing infirmities there is reason to fear a relapse, and the consequences of a second attack".

The news of Mrs Thompson's seizure reached her husband on 31st January. Much better reports were posted on 28th January, both by Philothea and by Miss Eliza Foster, who is not previously mentioned but "is with them at Penzance".

"On 31st January", Thompson then wrote, "the favourable account was repeated. *But Alas!* In the night of 1st February my dear Wife had a second attack of apoplexy, and expired about 3 o'clock on the morning of 2nd February 1823, and on Thursday 6th February I received the afflicting news from Mr Giddy of Penzance"[1].

Philothea was with her mother when it happened, probably assisted by Miss Foster. John may have been called to his mother's bedside: I do not know. By strange coincidence, Mrs Thompson's son Thomas landed in England on the day she died. He had arrived home from India with Nancy, after a journey, much of it overland, which had lasted more than a year[6,69]. "I shall probably see Thomas no more in this world", his mother had written in 1814, when he sailed for India; "but I shall be perfectly content if I have reason to hope for a joyful meeting in a better world". She always pinned her hopes on the 'land o' the leal'.

The principal Cornish newspaper, the 'West Briton', gave what information it could on 14th February: "At her lodgings at Penzance, where she had been to avoid the great severity of the season at her usual residence in Yorkshire, Mrs Thompson, wife of --- Thompson Esq"[87]. The funeral, conducted by the Vicar of Gulval, was on Saturday 15th February[31], nearly two weeks after her death. No doubt it gave relatives the opportunity to attend. That took time. The news took four days to reach her husband. A mail coach timetable of 1836 (no doubt it was similar in 1823) shows that somebody leaving Hull on the morning of Monday 10th, travelling on main roads via London, could probably reach Penzance on the morning of Thursday 13th — if they were willing to spend three consecutive nights in coaches[13].

It could not have been a wise journey for Thomas Thompson; and his journal shows that he remained at Cottingham. He tried to find a glimpse of Providence in his wife's death, but the entry written on 8th February shows the effort to do so. "I am unable to draw a character of this excellent woman until it shall please God to bring my mind to a more settled confidence in his wisdom, providence and grace, and enable me to say, 'Thou hast dealt well with thy servant, O Lord'. Thou hast dealt well with the husband, and well with the wife, and most merciful Father, deal well with their *children*, and save them everlastingly!"[1]

"Before the Rev Thomas Kelk delivered a Funeral Sermon for my dear Wife in Waltham Street Chapel, Hull", Thompson wrote later, "I drew up a short account of my wife's religious experience which is now in the hands of my dear daughter Philothea, and may be copied here [i.e. in his journal] at a future date". Unfortunately that account has not survived, so it is good to know that "my dear Wife remembered, when on her death bed at Penzance", the lines which Charles Wesley composed just before his own death:
'In age and feebleness extreme
Who shall a sinful worm redeem?
Jesus, my only hope thou art,
Strength of my failing flesh and heart;
O! could I catch a smile from thee
And drop into Eternity!'[1]

In the following two months Thompson seems to have partly occupied his mind by observing the Keldgate Springs, which were overflowing for the second successive year. "There has been much snow this year, and its gradual thaw on the Wolds may have raised the Springs". He had three men digging 'chalk-stone' in the north part of his grounds. The diggings were in the form of a cave in a hillside, and he watched the men working by candlelight, bringing out six tons of chalk per day, for which he paid one shilling per ton (two shillings per day for each man). He observed the chalk, marle, fuller's earth and pockets of gravel which were uncovered by the excavation, and thought "it may afford some amusement to the geologist". Early in April, ten of his sheep died of 'the black water' from eating a certain sort of turnip, and his servant, Richard

Hall, moved the rest of the flock to safety on other ground. Spring began to dry out the wet pastures: "the verdure is delightful, and shows that the God of the seasons is about to cloath the earth in her most beautiful garments". "My kind sister Jane intends to come to me next week", wrote Thompson on 16th April, "and I hope to spend a great part of my time here [at Cottingham] in retirement, which both my body and mind much need"[1].

A month later, on 16th May, Philothea died in Penzance, and was buried at Gulval, on 28th May, by James Carne, Curate of Sancreed[31]. Mrs Opie describes the two deaths in her poem 'On a Mother and Daughter, Relations of mine, who died at Penzance within a short time of each other'. In the poem, Philothea gives instructions to those digging her mother's grave:

"'Go! make her grave," she said, "and make
    it wide!
I soon shall slumber by my mother's side." '[52]

Whether Philothea spoke the words or not, she must have had the premonition; and so, as her niece Isabel Sidgwick wrote, "they lie side by side in the little churchyard of Gulval, within sound of the sea and in sight of St Michael's Mount". Philothea is reported to have been loved by Thomas Turton, a Hull man, Cambridge don[6] and friend of her brother Thomas[2], who later became Bishop of Ely, but who was felt by Thomas Thompson to be unsuitable for his daughter[6]. "I do not know that the serenity of our gentle saint-like Aunt was ruffled by any wishes in this direction", her niece went on. "I only know that he came and went, and I have fancied that if she had been made some good man's joy, her life would have been richer, and might have been happier"[4]. The monument to mother and daughter at Gulval church looks beyond all that. "The two sick strangers will now feel pain and sorrow no more", it reads; "and are blessed with the dead that die in the Lord"[30].

I hope that at least some relatives and friends were with Philothea at the time of her death. It seems almost impossible that they were not; but there are no records on the matter. The next reference is in her father's journal, written at Cottingham on 30th June, reflecting that, although he has been brought low, he is aware of God's mercy. That is his theme the next time that he writes in that journal, on 25th December. Unusually, both for himself and his wife, he takes up the specific theme of Christmas. "For all the mercies which I enjoy, I would on this day, Christmas Day 1823, give 'Glory to God in the highest' ", he writes. Then he turns to the thought of "dying Saints". "It was wise in a dying Father", he writes, "to desire that his Children would continue to read to him the promise of God, until they were certain that his spirit had left the body. When on my death bed, I hope that my Sons, my Sisters, or some friend who may be near me, will read to me the Word of God, so long as I appear to *breathe*". "The following promises have been precious to me", was his final entry for the year 1823: and he listed on that page, or added later with another pen, some thirty 'promises' from the Epistles of the New Testament, the book of Psalms, and the book of the prophet Isaiah[1].

CHAPTER 21

A tower with a view
1824-1826

ON 14TH FEBRUARY 1824, Thompson described himself at Cottingham, spending a few hours each day in managing the grounds round the Castle. "In wooden clogs, and a great coat, and a prod or small spade in my hand, I find no great inconvenience from the winds". His servant Richard was feeding Thompson's 300 sheep on turnips, and bringing the ewes to the fold yard, "that they may be better attended in dropping their lambs in the night"[1].

That is in his agricultural notes. A week later he wrote, in his main journal, of how he had attempted, on several occasions, "to collect the memorials of the death of my dear Wife and Daughter, in hopes that they may be of some religious benefit to my Sons or their children, and that they may not be thrown away as waste paper". The 'memorials' were principally written by friends, but he would add to them himself, he said, "as soon as I can attain firmness of mind sufficient to enable me to enter into a description of the character of the dear departed Saints who have left me to sojourn a few more days on earth". The use of 'death' and 'character' in the singular, in describing both his wife and daughter, suggests that he thought of them as very much united.

As he attended to business, and to work for the needy, he found himself very weak. "In the discussion of various subjects of business and beneficence, and in walking through various parts of the town", he wrote in March, "I find that by three o'clock my breath is short, my knees feeble, and my strength so much reduced that I am glad to throw myself into an armchair". A month later, however, he attended missionary meetings at Cottingham, Beverley and Welton on three successive, and successful, days. One of the preachers, Dr Bogue, observed that from the year 1580 to that time, not one country, province or even city, in Europe, had been added to the protestant communion. "Let the Methodists dwell on this fact, and take warning", wrote Thompson; and the next month he himself urged a Methodist meeting in Hull" to 'Go and teach all nations', and to expect Christ to fulfil the promise, 'Lo, I am with you always'[1].

At about this time his son Thomas visited him, and left Nancy and the children to stay at the Castle when he rejoined his regiment in Kent. The 17th Light Dragoons became the '17th Light Dragoons (Lancers)' in 1824; and officers of Lancers wore a heavy moustache. It was an adornment rarely worn by civilians at the time, and an unusual sight in Yorkshire. "Captain Thompson", wrote that officer's grand-daughter in later years, "was of a retiring disposition, and thought it necessary, on going down into his native wilds, to shave off his moustache, as making him too conspicuous, and savouring too much of military arrogance"[69].

That June, Thomas Thompson published his 'History of the Church and Priory of Swine', a book of 260 pages, priced at twelve shillings[75]. 'Some persons who know the parish may read it with avidity', he wrote

in his journal in August. The book makes good reading today, not least because of the author's frankness. Whilst, as he says in the Preface, he has 'no wish to disguise his own sentiments as a protestant', he does not condemn the pre-Reformation convent of Swine, whose life he decribes in some detail. Rather he castigates the sixteenth century Reformers who destroyed buildings 'more with the appearance of sacrilegious revenge than of pious zeal for the advancement of religion'. Furthermore, he strongly rebukes the 'ignorant churchwardens' and 'ignorant workmen' who had altered the tower of Swine church, removed ancient glass windows, and made ancient tombstones into 'stepping stones for the horsing block at the entrance of the churchyard' during his own lifetime. 'It has been justly observed that the congruity of Gothic architecture is so complete that it allows of no admixture of modern invention', says Thompson. 'When we hear of great improvements about to be made in a Gothic church by country churchwardens and country builders, we have reason to tremble, as we may be certain that some irreparable mischief is at hand'.

However, he admits, there is "tedium in local history", so he gives further details of village life. He notes, for example, that because people were averse to burial on the north side of churches, a felon executed sixty years before — when Thompson was a youth — had been buried on that side of Swine church. Again, when he was a youth, the ceremony of walking the parish boundaries, or 'perambulation', consisted of a prayer under an oak tree and a distribution of bread rolls and ale to the village boys. "This was called, in provincial language, 'Swine ramble-ation', and was a very noisy ramble indeed", writes Thompson. Even at the time when he was writing, 1824, the feast of the patron saint still caused "much disorder, which the magistrates have not been able to suppress'; and on midsummer eve 'the boys of Swine make a large fire near the [village] cross, and sometimes continue to hollow and play around it till midnight"[75].

It is all of interest to us today. However, Thompson noted in his journal that August, his interest in the village of his birth had led him to spend longer on this book than he had intended. "I am not convinced that I ought to spend my time in what is called 'innocent employment' ", he told himself. "This is often a *waste* of time, and therefore becomes sinful".

More "fulness in the head, and sometimes alarming swimming or giddiness" followed that month, with more bleeding, and instructions to eat very little meat, and to drink only water. (The medical regime which had been applied to Princess Charlotte[58], with fatal results, was very widespread). He was not greatly concerned to prolong his life, however, and he added a reminder, in his journal, of where his will and a list of bequests could be found. That month he wrote, "I am weary of farming". He had let most of the Castle's farm land to tenants, and would just retain the plantations of young trees near the house. He suspected that a tenant farmer would not look after those, and would probably "suffer his cattle to destroy them all"[1].

Withdrawing from broader acres to the vicinity of the Castle (where he watched "the hounds of my neighbour Wilkinson pursue a poor hare", and determined that the huntsmen should not follow with their horses), he embarked, in fact, on fresh activities. "I am employing three poor labourers to raise the hill at the western extremity of the West Park, and to form the sides into different circular terraces", he wrote in December. Soon he began to plan the last of his buildings, to stand on the "western extremity" of what are now the Castle Hill Hospital grounds. "Suppose a Tower on the Hill at Cottingham, with something like the following inscription", he wrote in February 1825. "What would be the expence of the building?"

His proposed inscription ran:-
Ut Humbrem ut Terram
undique beatam videas
Amice
haec Turris de longis
spectabilis sumptibus
T.T.

Thomas Thompson's 'Prospect Tower', built in 1825. The only building surviving from Cottingham Castle.

PHOTOGRAPH BY THE AUTHOR

anno Domini 1825
extructa fuit

'Friend, this Tower, with its wide view, was built in 1825 at Thomas Thompson's expense, for you to see the Humber and the lovely land on every side'. A builder, Mr Mennell, began it that June, charging £200 for the work. Inside, at the top, there was to be a table with a map identifying all the places which could be seen, and "suitable extracts from our best poets" — Cowper and Goldsmith were among them — "as subjects of profitable conversation to the persons who visit the Prospect Tower"[1]. The tower stands in a little wood today, the last surviving building from Cottingham Castle. It is sometimes called the 'folly', which is something of a misnomer for a building as purposefully designed as this was. The entrance is bricked up, so I do not know whether Thompson's inscription was ever carved inside.

In that year, 1825, at the age of seventy one, he was still involved with the Hull bank. He senior clerk wrote to London in that year to convey Thompson's comments on the South American republics — Chile, Peru, Gran Colombia — which had recently become independent from Spain. "There has not been much time to judge of the stability of the governments in South America, and Mr Thompson thinks that it is very possible that there may be various quarrels amongst them for territory or preponderancy, encouraged by old Spain: but he has no objection to your purchasing £5000 of the Stock you mention"[7]. He was quite right to foresee both the quarrels, and the opportunities for trade and commerce, in that part of the world. He must have known of them at least since 1806, when his son Thomas was at Buenos Aires with the Rifles.

In August 1825 he had "fullness in the head" again. "I should prefer Dr Alderson to any other", he wrote, "but as I do not suppose the case is difficult, I have sent for Mr W., the surgeon and apothecary of Cottingham" (perhaps the same as Mr Watson, previously mentioned). In the event, "Mr G., a partner of Mr W." bled him, and prescribed an aperient of 'alkaline and acid, something like a Seidlitz powder"[1].

In the next month, September 1825, Thomas Thompson and Dr Alderson, both of them widowers, were no doubt present when Thompson's son John married Alderson's daughter Margaret at Sculcoates Parish Church. John was forty years old; his bride twenty six. In due course eight children followed. An illustration in this book shows Margaret Thompson with their eldest child, Philothea Margaret, on her knee. The portrait is by Henry Perronet Briggs, who was related both to John and to his wife, and whose father, John Hobart Briggs, had been a witness at the runaway wedding of Thomas Thompson to Nancy[6]. A further illustration shows Amelia Opie, who had taken young Margaret Alderson to the victory celebration in London in 1814, and who in that year, 1825, became a member of the Society of Friends, or Quakers. The illustration shows her in the style of Quaker bonnet associated with Elizabeth Fry the prison reformer; but Mrs Opie's bonnet, true to its owner, was always as trim as a Quaker lady was permitted to wear[4].

In May 1826 Thomas Thompson recorded that, that year, the distresses in the commercial world had been greater than he could ever remember. More than one hundred country banks had "stopt payment", and many London banks had failed too, unable to meet demands for gold. Bank customers of Sir Peter Pole & Co, and of Wentworth Chaloner & Rishworth of York, had particularly suffered. Thompson maintained close touch with his own Bank in Hull. He had "been preserved from corroding anxiety", he said, "by always having enough in the *Chest*, not with a miser's delight, but with the satisfaction that I could pay the debts of the Bank as fast as they could be demanded, and that I could replenish the Chest with Gold from London when necessary"[1].

His son Thomas, now a major in the Army, with Nancy and their four children, visited him at Cottingham Castle in July. The children had "natural abilities", wrote their grandfather, and he hoped that they would give happiness to society and to their parents, "especially if it shall please God to implant the fear of

God in their hearts". Meanwhile, he did think that Thomas and Nancy were rather too indulgent with their offspring. John and his wife Margaret were also visiting the Castle. All these people filled up the bedrooms, and Thompson noted, not for the first time, that "I have scarcely room for many visitants at once". His eldest grandson Perronet sometimes visited on his own, however, coming on Saturdays from Pocklington Grammar School. "Partly to please him", partly to water his cattle, and partly, no doubt, as an interesting project, Thompson built a fish pond in front of the Castle that October. It must be well planned, he reminded himself. "The directions under the title 'Fish Ponds' in the Cyclopedia, and in 'Daniel's' Rural Sports' must be studied and followed"[1].

That autumn in Cottingham he often worked outside until he perspired profusely, believing that that would prevent fullness of blood in the head. When winter came, he said, it would have to be prevented by bleeding. As autumn drew on he noted that three corn millers in Cottingham were in the habit of grinding corn on the Sabbath, but that the Vicar and Churchwardens made no protest. One Sunday in November, therefore, "I called one of the Millers out of his Mill, and reasoned with him on his conduct, as being contrary to the laws of God and man, and mentioned his liability to be fined on complaint being made to a Magistrate". That miller, and the other two, gave up their Sunday grinding. If there was no wind during the week, Thompson believed, a man might grind on the Sabbath, in order to supply the people with bread; "but such a case can rarely happen".

Early in December he went to Hull for the winter months. It was convenient to be at the Bank at Christmas time, he said, and easier to attend worship in Hull than in Cottingham. "In the winter I am unable to ride from the Castle to the Chapel at Cottingham, but at Hull I am so near the Chapel in George Yard than I can walk there without much pain from the want of breath".

The type of revival which Methodists often demonstrated could sometimes be found in the Church of England; and men like Thompson, who worshipped with both congregations, could observe it. In December 1826 he wrote about the Church of England, whose beautiful Litany was in danger of becoming meaningless from thoughtless repetition. "Many who have repeated the prayers in the Litany a thousand times without feeling their *mercy*, are now praying, with broken hearts and contrite spirits, 'Lord have mercy upon us' ", he said. It was the Methodists, however, who were particularly associated with revival. That Christmas Eve the Waltham Street Chapel, one of the largest Methodist Chapels in England, was completely filled for a Love Feast. "Many had walked from very distant places in the county, and some who had walked all the preceding night could only find a standing [sic] in the aisles". There were enough Methodists to fill the place by themselves, said Thompson, but many 'Dissenters' had come to join them too; so it was decided to postpone the Love Feast until Christmas Day afternoon, and to restrict it to members of Methodist societies. On Christmas Day afternoon it was full again. The revival seemed to be principally among young men and women, Thompson noted: but "many old backsliders were lamenting their backslidings" as well[1].

Another Methodist ceremony, the Watchnight, was held at George Street Chapel on New Year's Eve, with preaching, exposition and prayer from 9 p.m. until midnight, then a hymn, and then a return home. It was a wonderful time, wrote Thompson. "The people come up to the house of God in troops. The preachers preach Eternity, and the people hear, and God is in the midst of the congregations". "In a religious view, this year, 1826, ends gloriously among the Methodists at Hull", he said[1]. He hoped that the Methodist ministers were keeping some record of it all; but perhaps some of the best descriptions were written by himself.

CHAPTER 22

No silent sliding away
1827-1828

IN THE YEAR 1827 Thomas Perronet Thompson, now reaching the political stage of his career, published his 'Catechism of the Corn Law'. Still a major in the Army at the time, he expounded a strong anti-Corn Law position by means of a 'catechism' of imaginary questions to which he supplied his own pungent answers. He is rightly remembered for the concise and witty style of this booklet, which is still enjoyable to read today, and in his later publications such as the 'Catholic State Waggon'. I myself thought that the style was his own until I read Thomas Thompson's speeches in Hansard, and realised how much the use of homely illustrations and telling phrases had passed from father to son.

In 1827, too, John Vincent Thompson was appointed Recorder of Beverley, the last holder of that ancient office in the town[55]. The Recorder was not required to live in Beverley, but to attend its Council "on grave and extraordinary occasions which demand the presence of a legal adviser", and "at Quarter Sessions where criminals are arraigned before juries"[50]. For most of the year, presumably, John's work as a barrister was in London or on circuit. He may have owned a house in Beverley, however. A 'John Thompson, attorney' is recorded both at North Bar Within and at Toll Gavel in the Beverley directory of 1826[14]. Outside the town gate, or Bar, a fashionable quarter was growing up in North Bar Without. The law court, built in 1810, still functions there beneath the combined arms of Britain and Hanover; and behind the handsome houses there still stands, incongruously, the remains of the penitentiary for men, women and children, which was built at the same time.

The ledgers of Smiths & Thompson's banks in Hull, now preserved with the archives of the National Westminster Bank in London, were extensively researched by Leighton-Boyce in his study of the various Smith family banks. They also provide much information about Thompson's own business connections and banking customers. Suffice it to say here that they include, under names familiar from this narrative, various accounts held by William Wilberforce; by the Hull Dock Company; and by the Methodist Missionary Society. Under Thomas Thompson's own account, in those years, we find payments to his sister Mrs Anne Wainewright, apparently of £105 per year, and payments to his sister Miss Jane Thompson which, at one time at least, were for £50 per month. Jane Thompson may sometimes have looked after his grandson Perronet, as payments to "Miss Thompson, for Perronet" appear in 1824 and 1826. There is a payment of £1000 to his son Thomas ("Major Thompson") in 1826, and another of £50 to John's wife ("Mrs J.V. Thompson") in 1827[63].

On 5th January 1828, a date sometimes called Old Christmas Day, Thomas Thompson, aged seventy four, finally gave up control of the Hull bank. Documents in the National Westminster archives show that the partners of Smiths and Thompson's made regular partnership agreements. The 1818 agreement shows that the "capital employed by the Bank" had been advanced to it by the partners in the following proportions: Samuel Smith of Woodhall Park, Hertfordshire, four twentyfourths; George Smith of Upper Harley Street, Middlesex, three twentyfourths; John Smith of New Street, Spring Gardens, Westminster, four twenty-fourths; Thomas Thompson of Kingston Upon Hull, nine twentyfourths; and Oswald Smith of Kingston Upon Hull, four twentyfourths. On Thomas Thompson's retirement in 1828, £60,668.2.7. was paid by the new partners to the old[63]; Thompson's nine twenty-fourths of that, nearly £23,000, presumably indicating that that amount of his own capital had been made available for the bank's use.

The last piece of Thomas Thompson's handwriting which I have read, on other than business matters, is about the Christian churches. In September 1827 he writes in his journal: "Religion among the Methodists is not a silent sliding into an unfeeling approbation of Gospel truth ... It is the power of God in the soul ... This spiritual and new life is not dastardly or dormant, but is faithful and awake in God's service". He had heard that some Methodist ministers would like the Church of England service read in the Methodist chapel, "previous to the preaching". Thompson, who had always held high hopes of the Anglican church, now believed that that would introduce "formality, care-lessness and sleepy dullness" among Methodists. "Persons who desire to have the Church prayers read", he observes, "are quite at liberty to attend the Church [of England] service, if they can keep their attention fixed, and can earnestly pray during so long a service (often read with as little devotion as the reading of a Newspaper). The Methodists will thank God on their account. But it is not by a long form of prayer, however good, that God carries on his work among the Methodists. Their preachers pray with the Spirit, and with the Understanding ... and cry mightily and instantly to God for the blessings which their people need, and feel they need *now*; and from which they

ought not to be diverted by a careless reader, in vain repetitions of words, or by a useless voluntary on the organ"[1]. Once more, and on the closing page of his journal, he contrasts unreality with reality.

In the summer of 1828, Thompson went abroad, for the first time in his life. Poulson in the last century[56], and Johnson in this[6], say that he went for antiquarian studies in Normandy. After reading his journals, I would like to know the reason more clearly. He was, after all, seventy four years old and not at all well. France was the country he had spoken against most strongly for infidelity and immorality. It was the country of unbelieving philosophers: the country where both his son John and his friend Lord Carrington sojourned at their peril. Just 'antiquarian research' does not seem reason enough for the journey. Perhaps he had it in mind to take some Protestant influence there, as he had hoped others would. Perhaps he wished to visit the country where Charles had been killed, and was buried.

Johnson says that he was accompanied by his "two eldest grandchildren"[6], who were Lucy and Perronet, aged sixteen and fifteen. If, as seems possible, a girl of that age would not have travelled unchaperoned, the two eldest grandsons were Perronet and Charles. Whoever was with him, Thompson was taken ill at Rouen. He was moved to Paris for treatment, and died there, at Meurice's Hotel, on 14th September 1828.

John was with him when he died. I would like to think that he knew, and complied with, the wish which his father had written in his journal on the Christmas Day after Mrs Thompson and Philothea died: "When on my death bed, I hope that my Sons, my Sisters, or some friend who may be near me, will read to me the Word of God, so long as I appear to breathe"[1]. Thomas, stationed in Ireland, was sent the news, and wrote to Nancy in York. "I shall never direct a letter to 'Bank, Hull' again", he said. "I did not think I loved the Bank much. But it is the breaking up of five and forty years' recollections"[6].

Under the terms of his will, dated 27th May 1824,

almost everything went to Thompson's surviving sons, Thomas and John. Several pieces of land were involved: Thomas received the estate at Cottingham, and also land at Patrington, Patrington Haven and Hollym, and in Holderness. John received land at Ryehill, Thorngumbald and Elsternwick, all in Holderness. £5000 was invested to provide a lifetime income for Thomas Thompson's sister, Mrs Anne Wainewright, whose son Thomas Thompson Wainewright was already dead. Miss Thompson, his "kind sister Jane", does not appear in the will, having perhaps had provision made for her already. £10,000 was invested for the grandchildren when each should reach the age of twenty one. The clerks at Smiths and Thompson's bank received £50 each, 'for mourning', and James Henwood (once described as assistant to the bank's junior partner, Oswald Smith, but now as 'James Henwood, merchant'), £150. Six of the Smith family — Robert (Lord Carrington), Samuel, George, John, Abel (son of Samuel) and Oswald (son of George) received £100 each "in grateful remembrance of their kindness and friendship"[76]. It was not a will which made bequests to charity. That may have been because Thompson made specific gifts, as need arose, in his lifetime. Another reason may be found in the list of requests which he recorded in his journal in 1817. These included certain gifts to chapels and Sunday schools, and generous provision for his servants, "both male and female": but they were gifts which he asked his sons to make from the money they inherited, as if to bring home to them that they had received much and were in a position to pass on some of it, not as an obligation but as an act of generosity[1].

He was buried in Paris, at Pére la Chaise cemetery. A week after the burial, the 'Hull Advertiser' of 26th September 1828 paid tribute to 'Thomas Thompson, Banker of this town':- "It has seldom fallen to our lot to record the death of an individual more highly respected for his talents and various excellencies than this lamented gentleman". A tablet was placed in Cottingham parish church, near that of his son Charles, "on the south side of the choir", as he had wished. It records him as banker, and as Member for Midhurst in three successive parliaments. "Humility and the Fear of the Lord brought him prosperity", the inscription goes on; "and after a life of diligence in business, and active benevolence towards those who have none to help them, he committed his soul to God, who gave his Son to death to redeem him. He married Miss Philothea Perronet Briggs, of Hoxton Square, London, who died [in] 1823 at Penzance in Cornwall"[20].

The printed Minutes of the Methodist Conference of 1829 include a tribute to Thomas Thompson which particularly link him with Methodist missionary work, both in this country and overseas. After referring to Benson's influence on Thompson as a young man [since Joseph Benson did not come to Hull until 1786, the reference should perhaps have been to the influence of Joseph Milner], it says of Thompson that "by his exertions, a large district of country [Holderness], involved at that time in deep ignorance, and characterised by rude opposition to the Gospel, was brought under religious cultivation". Success in business, and prosperity, the account goes on, "had no effect in damping his zeal, or diminishing the force of a piety which retained its primitive character of simplicity and ardour through the whole period of an extended life". Referring to his wise influence in the time of confused church government which followed the death of John Wesley, it says that Thompson, resisting "the democratic and levelling politics of the day", was a leading instrument in effecting a "mutual recognition of rights and duties" by both ministers and congregations. Finally, this obituary recalls that Thompson chaired the first District Missionary Society meeting, at Leeds in 1813, and the first such meeting at Hull in the same year; "and they who had the happiness to be present at those meetings will remember, with the most lively feelings, the power with which he spoke" on those occasions which were so important for "promoting the conversion of the heathen to every Methodist society and congregation"[43].

Margaret Thompson (daughter of Dr John & Mrs Sarah Alderson and wife of John Vincent Thompson) and her daughter Philothea Margaret.

PORTRAIT BY HENRY PERRONET BRIGGS RA (1829) OWNED BY THE AUTHOR

102

This book has described the Thompsons, two parents and four children, as a family group, and it ends here, with the death of the second parent. Not one of the six who once lived together in Hull was buried there. Thomas Thompson lies in Paris; Mrs Thompson and Philothea in Cornwall; Charles near the border of France and Spain. Thomas and his wife Nancy, in due course, were buried at Kensal Green in London. John died at Torquay, in a house which is now the Osborne Hotel, near where his friend William Scoresby, whaling captain and clergyman, had gone to live. John and Margaret are buried in London.

Two of my illustrations show Thomas Perronet Thompson as a captain (he held the rank from 1814 until the mid-1820s), and John Vincent Thompson as a barrister of indeterminate age. Thomas, on his father's death, inherited Cottingham Castle, but never lived there. It was let to tenants until the main building was dramatically though accidentally destroyed by fire in 1861.

Thomas left active service in 1829, when he was forty six, buying an unattached lieutenant-colonelcy. (Further promotions took him to the rank of general, which he achieved in 1868, at the age of eighty five). No longer dependent on the Army for a living, he bought the 'Westminter Review', campaigned against the Corn Laws and for Catholic Emancipation, sat as a Radical member for Hull and later twice for Bradford (generally known as 'Colonel Thompson'), and invented an enharmonic organ which was shown at the Great Exhibition and is still in the Science Museum. Nancy continued to be his active companion. Two of their sons became soldiers: I have sketches which one of them made in the Crimean War. Their son Perronet, who had been brought up in Yorkshire while his parents were in India, and who had visited Scarborough with his barrister uncle John, became a judge. The judge's daughter Edith Thompson (died 1929), who knew Thomas Perronet Thompson as her interesting and always interested 'Grandpapa', collected and arranged his papers which are now in the University Libraries of Hull and Leeds.

John prospered as a barrister ("John sat at the Sessions with considerable éclat", his brother wrote in 1823). As a Serjeant at Law (appointed in 1841)[40], he is sometimes referred to as Mr Serjeant Thompson. He and his wife Margaret brought up eight children in London. They lived in Upper Belgrave Street, a street where the Duke of Wellington often came to visit his own son. "Every man used to 'cap' the Iron Duke", wrote one of John's sons, Vincent Thomas, in later years, "and they got an informal military salute in return"[5]. The same son recorded that the crowd would applaud the popular Marshal Soult, French Ambassador to Britain, when he arrived at nearby Apsley House for the annual Waterloo Banquet. It was more than thirty years since Charles had been killed when fighting Soult's troops in France.

John remained in touch with Hull, giving his support to the very successful Hull Mechanics' Institute which his father in law John Alderson had helped to found. He presented that Institute with an appropriate painting by his cousin Henry Perronet Briggs, 'The Romans instructing the Ancient Britons', and with a bust of Queen Victoria[97]. As one of the Treasurers of St George's Hospital, London[5], from 1833 to 1855[65], he knew the surgeon Benjamin Collins Brodie. In due course his daughter Philothea Margaret, shown in my illustration as a baby on her mother's knee, married Brodie's son, who was Professor of Chemistry in Oxford at the time of the 1860 'Origin of Species' debate. John and Margaret Thompson's son Vincent Thomas was sent to Rugby in 1851, in the last year of Thomas Arnold's headmastership. When John took the boy to school for his first term, it was the first time, remarkably, that the barrister had ever travelled by train. He was of the stage coach era, telling the same son of the need to put on two shirts when travelling on top of a coach in winter[5]; though in other ways, particularly through his letters, he seems quite modern. Those letters, to and from his mother, exist today through the care of one of his great granddaughters, Jessica Thompson. Family stories do not really come to an end.

POSTSCRIPT
"If God smiles upon me"

THOMAS THOMPSON AND HIS WIFE lived their lives against a background of changing events which has hardly been mentioned in this book. In the ten years before they were born, the Young Pretender was defeated at Culloden; Gray published his churchyard Elegy; and Handel wrote music for the royal fireworks. In the year of Thompson's birth, Chippendale published his directory of furniture; and the Royal Society of Arts ('for the Encouragement of Arts, Manufactures and Commerce') was founded. While Mr and Mrs Thompson were children — one in Yorkshire, one in London — Johnson published his Dictionary; Mozart was born; the first modern canal was cut, from St Helens to the Mersey; and Britain, by capturing Quebec, gained much of Canada. Whilst they were in their teens, numerous Enclosure Acts rearranged the land and its uses; Parliament authorised many miles of turnpike roads; and textile workers first encountered Hargreaves' spinning jenny and Arkwright's water frame. By the time the Thompsons were married, Watt and Boulton were applying steam to pumping engines and factory machinery; and the North American colonies had declared their independence. During their marriage, the French Revolution turned established ideas upside down; the first lives were saved by smallpox vaccination; very many more were lost in the long Napoleonic wars; and Britain returned to a troubled peace.

Thomas Thompson and his wife knew both town and country. He was born on a poor farm, but it was near Hull with its international trade. She grew up on the edge of the City of London, but that was near the countryside. Both of them travelled quite considerably in England. Both had wide interests, though inevitably the husband had far more opportunity to pursue them than his wife. Thompson's range of experience meant that he was not a farmer, immersed in problems of the land, yet he was very well informed about the countryside. He was not a professional politician, absorbed by the intrigues of Westminster, yet he promoted a whole range of causes in Parliament. He was not a clergyman, with a routine of ecclesiastical duties to perform, but he believed that he owed a debt to God.

Mr and Mrs Thompson's faith was a constant factor in their lives. Both had been influenced by the Wesleys. Mrs Thompson's parents, and Perronet grandparents, had continued that influence. Thomas Thompson knew Joseph Milner and perhaps Joseph Benson, when he was a young man, and the Clapham Sect in later years. "I have been a child of Providence from my birth until now", he wrote when he was sixty. "The designs of my parents concerning me appear to have been inspired by Providence; and when I left the place of my birth, Providence appointed me friends, and many of them, with minds filled with Christian love and grace"[1]. Each of those people — Thompson, his wife and their believing friends — saw the need for men and women to accept Christ as their own Saviour, as later generations would put it. William Wilberforce called it "the great change''[54], and looked for it in his children, as the Thompsons did in theirs.

Those who underwent that "change" were not expected to sit down and rejoice, but to apply the gift which they had received to all their circumstances. In the case of Thomas Thompson those circumstances were very wide indeed. It is easy to forget, among his other activities, that he was an active merchant, and still more active banker, throughout his life. In those spheres he endeavoured to combine natural talent and energy with sound and honest principles which protected his customers as well as his firm and its partners. His life in Hull expanded in one direction to the development of the Docks, and in another direction to feeding the poor adequately, at a price which ratepayers could accept. A countryman by birth, he explained the advantages of tithe reform both to farmers and clergy; and he promoted the self-sufficiency of the poor by allocating them their own land. In Parliament, he spoke knowledgeably and often pungently on subjects as important, and diverse, as proper wages for labourers; treatment of the insane; the prices of corn and of bread; the needs of children in factories; the choice between gold coin and bank notes; the morality of State lotteries; the protection of Yorkshire fishermen; the promotion of education in India; the government's need to control its spending; and the proper approach to demonstrators and to forgers. In addition to all this, Thompson was known as a tireless promoter of religious teaching, both in this country and abroad.

I hope that the many solemn subjects and occasions in this book have not obliterated the humour which each of the Thompsons showed. It is often demonstrated in the letters of the children, Thomas, John, Charles and Philothea. It is there, though surrounded by many serious thoughts, in Mrs Thompson's letters. It is certainly in Thomas Thompson's speeches in the House of Commons. He and his wife, however, are bound to be remembered for their purposefulness more than for their gaiety. (The point was made by Wilberforce at the time of Charles' death). The urgency of the evangelical message, and its demands upon those who hear it, will always make some listeners turn away, hesitating to make any public claim to their own salvation.

An active faith proclaims that God is active. Thompson and his wife sometimes expressed this activity as 'providence' (the word is included in my index). Mrs Thompson trusted that providence would assist matters in Sierra Leone, and questioned whether providence would really send John to India. Providence, of course, is not predestination. Predestination constrains; providence equips. Thompson expressed that in 1815, when he wrote: "I might adopt the motto, 'God's Providence, mine Inheritance', as I had no other heritage, all the property being dissipated which I had reason to expect, and my Family [in Swine] reduced to a state of dependence on my own exertions. But, 'Hitherto the Lord hath helped' "[1].

Providence sometimes seemed stern, but it had another aspect too. 'Behind a frowning providence, God hides a smiling face', wrote William Cowper. Mrs Thompson liked to think of God's 'smile' during her last days in Cornwall[1]. Thompson's journal of 1824 takes up the same theme. When Isaac Watts died in 1748, he noted, Benjamin Grosvenor, a Dissenting minister, was at the funeral. ' "Well, Dr Grosvenor", said a friend, "you have seen the end of Dr Watts, and you will soon follow. What think you of death?" "Think of it?", replied the Doctor. "Why, when death comes I shall smile upon it, if God smiles upon me" '[1].

Faith, openly expressed, in a God who not only provides but often 'smiles', is not for everybody. Thus none of the Thompsons' sons, to my knowledge, made claim to the particular faith of their parents, although Philothea did. I believe, nevertheless, that the parents' principles emerge in the lives of their sons, Thomas and John, who survived them. They bore fruit, for example, in Thomas Perronet Thompson's courageous administration of Sierra Leone while still a young man (*"He did right"*, as James Stephen wrote, even while disagreeing with that administration)[2]; and in his incisive writing against the Corn Laws which his father had supported for opposite reasons. John Vincent Thompson expressed some of his father's wish to educate, and to administer money wisely, in his work for the Hull Mechanics' Institute and for St George's Hospital, London. "He [John] was a very abstemious man", wrote a grandson. "He breakfasted on a roll and tea, had no lunch, and dined at 6 p.m."[5]. We know all too little about John's forty years as a barrister and Serjeant at Law, in courts up and down the country; but perhaps he sometimes recalled the letter which his mother sent him when he qualified at the Bar in 1813. He certainly kept it, because it still survives, wishing him "Competence; friends; health; progressive virtue; and approving heaven".

Appendix:
The Account Book of Thomas Thompson's Executors

This Appendix, with its references to citizens of Hull and Cottingham, may be of particular interest to residents of those places today. The names mentioned are not included in the general index unless they already appear in the book.

Mr Benedict Thompson-McCausland kindly lent me a ledger, entitled "An Account of the Receipts and Payments of the Executors of the late Thomas Thompson Esqre., Septemr. 19th 1828"[32]. The entries in the ledger are by one of the executors, James Henwood.

This book gives details of Thompson's death which are not recorded elsewhere. For example, "Thomas Thompson Esqre. died at Paris on Sunday night Septemr. 14th 1828. He left Hull on Thursday morning July 17th 1828 intending to make a few weeks' Tour in France with part of his Family". "The tidings of Mr Thompson's death reached Hull on Friday Evening 19th Septemr. 1828".

The accounts show that soon after those "tidings", 83 lambs from Cottingham Castle were sold to Burgess the butcher for 14 shillings each; Thomas Shields the footman was reimbursed £1.6.10., the balance of his travelling expenses from Paris; Thompson's sister Jane received £19.11.4. to pay the servants' wages at the Castle; and John Vincent Thompson was reimbursed £52.0.0. for his father's funeral expenses in Paris.

It seems that Thomas Thompson's wishes concerning his servants, recorded in his journal several years before, were observed. He had wished them to be paid their wages for the remainder of the year in which he should die, and an extra year's wages besides. This account book shows that Thomas Shields the footman received £3.15/- balance of wages, presumably from his master's death to the end of 1828, and a gratuity of £15.15/-. Betty the housekeeper at Cottingham Castle got the same amount. Richard Hall was due 7 months' wages and received £30.16/-. He had a proportionately smaller gratuity of £29.8/-, but perhaps, as farm manager, he received some goods in kind. Jane West received a gratuity of £10.10/-, which indicates that that was her annual wage.

Thompson's partners duly received their £100 legacy each, from which 10% legacy tax was deducted, while D.G. Horwood, Henry Towse, John Linton, and James Henwood himself received £50 each, also less 10% tax. Rather invidiously, the much larger cash legacy of £1000 each to Thompson's sons Thomas and John was apparently only subject to 1% tax. Thomas Perronet Thompson, recorded in the ledger as 'Major T.P. Thompson' in November 1828, is shown as 'Colonel T.P. Thompson' in July 1829, indicating that he had bought his promotion by the later date.

Mourning was duly observed. Miss Jane Thompson was paid £24.1.6. for purchasing "mourning for Servants, etc.", and Mrs Pick was paid £2.2/- for "making mourning". Scarves and gloves, presumably of the mourning variety, were separately purchased for

£19.15/- and £2.16.6. respectively. In December 1828, James Henwood wrote to John Vincent Thompson: "I have given no directions for mourning Rings. They can be better got in London than through a Goldsmith here. I think the parties here to whom they should be sent are about twenty in number. I suppose they will cost 50/- each". In due course, Rundell Bridge & Co. were paid £90.10/- for mourning rings.

The total value of the "furniture, books, plate etc. at the Castle" was computed at £1770.9/-.

One entry in the accounts indicates that Thompson still remembered his native village, though the payment seems rather overdue: "Paid, Rent of Swine Cottage as a Preaching House to Lady Day [25 March] 1828, £1.17/-".

The following is a list of all the persons, other than servants, with whom the executors settled accounts:-

Alsop (supplier of 'scarfs etc'); Blaine & Co. ('scarfs etc'); Burgess (butcher — purchased Thompson's lambs); Bursell (carter? — paid toll money for 'leading materials'); Carr (brewer, Cottingham); Cussons (shoemaker); Davies (bookseller); Dossor (brewer); Ferraby (bookseller?); Fox & West (supplied building bricks); Frost (lawyer); Gee (supplier of gloves); Hebblewhite & Son (wool merchants); Hendry & Hyde (valuers of furniture); Hudson & Son (supplier of 'scarfs etc'); Huzzard (purchased a pony); Martin (nurseryman, Cottingham); Milson (supplier of building sand, Cottingham); Mountain (supplier of building slate); Palmer (wine merchant); Pick, Mrs (maker of mourning); Pudsey (tailor); Radford & Co. (booksellers?); Reynolds (bookseller?); Richardson (corn factor); Rundell Bridge & Co., London (suppliers of mourning rings); Smith (blacksmith, Cottingham); Turner & Co. (booksellers & stationery); Wardell (chaise hire); Wilson, Isaac (paid for 'appraising books'); Wride (joiner).

Bibliography & Other Sources

Reference numbers in the text relate to the source numbers below.

* = Direct descendant of Thomas Thompson.

PRIMARY SOURCES (listed in order of importance to this book)

1. Thomas Thompson, manuscript journals, years 1817-1827. Property of *Mr Martin Thompson.
2. Sixty original family letters, 1795-1821, principally from Philothea Perronet Thompson to her son John. Assembled by *Miss Jessica Thompson.
3. Hansard, 'Parliamentary Debates: House of Commons', years 1807-1818.
4. Family papers, mainly of *Miss Edith Thompson (1848-1929), including recollections by *Mrs Isabella Sidgwick. Property of the author.
5. *Herbert William Thompson (1874-1953), 'Notes on the Thompson family' written in 1943.
6. L.G. Johnson, 'General T. Perronet Thompson 1783-1865' (George Allen & Unwin 1957).
7. J.A.S.L. Leighton-Boyce, 'Smiths the Bankers 1658-1958' (National Provincial Bank 1958).

SECONDARY SOURCES (listed alphabetically)

8. Acland A.H.D. & Ransome C., 'A handbook of English political history' (Longmans 1909).
9. Ainsworth J., 'The Scarborough guide', 5th & 6th editions (1818 & 1820).
9a. Alderson, Dr James, declaration (1865) re marriage & children of his sister and J.V. Thompson, in Brynmor Jones Library, Hull, ref. DAS/7/33.
10. 'Bailey's Northern Directory' (1781) & 'Bailey's British Directory' (1784).
11. Baker F., 'John Wesley and the Church of England' (Epworth 1970).
12. Barker & Wycliffe families — information from various sources.
13. Bates A., 'Directory of stage coach services, 1836' (Augustus Kelley 1969).
14. Beverley — town directory, 1826.
15. Beverley Minster registers, in Humberside County Record Office.
16. Bickford J.A.R. & M.E., 'The medical profession in Hull 1400-1900' (Kingston upon Hull 1983).
17. Blackburn, Joseph — Trial of Joseph Blackburn, 1815 (contemporary account).
18. Blackstone W., 'Commentaries on the laws of England' (1822 edition).
19. Calvert H., 'A history of Hull' (Phillimore 1978).
20. Cottingham parish church — memorial inscriptions.
21. Court W.H.B., 'A concise economic history of Britain' (C.U.P. 1962).
22. Cumbers F., 'The Book Room: the story of the Methodist publishing house' (Epworth 1956).
23. *Dictionary of National Biography* entries for: Joseph Benson; William Briggs; Bowdler family; Carne family; Thomas Coke; William Dealtry; Charles James Fox; William Hey; Simon le

Blanc; Thomas Middleton; Isaac Milner; Robert Owen; Vincent Perronet; James Scarlett; Sarah Siddons; Dugald Stewart.

24. Dykes J., 'Smuggling on the Yorkshire Coast' (Dalesman Books 1978).

25. Emery A., 'A short history of Methodism in Cottingham' (1972, unpublished).

26. Gillett E. & MacMahon K.A., 'A history of Hull' (University of Hull 1980).

27. Green K.A., 'Old Cottingham revisited' (Hutton Press 1988).

28. Green, Dr Kenneth & Mrs Eileen — local information on Cottingham and on Thomas Thompson.

29. Gulval parish church — memorial inscriptions.

30. Gulval parish registers, in Cornwall Record Office.

31. Hamilton F.W., 'The origin & history of the First or Grenadier Guards' (John Murray 1874), and information from Regimental Archivist.

32. Henwood J., — manuscript accounts (1828-9) kept by executors of Thomas Thompson. Property of Mrs H. Thompson-McCausland.

33. Hooper W.E., 'History of Newgate & the Old Bailey' (Underwood Press 1935).

34. House of Commons — information from Public Information Office, House of Commons.

35. Hull Docks Museum — information from Keeper of Maritime History.

36. Jackson G., 'Hull in the eighteenth century: a study in economic & social history' (University of Hull 1972).

37. Johnson L.G., 'Thomas Thompson' — lecture to Cottingham Local History Society (1958, believed unpublished).

38. 'Law Times', 20th December 1856.

39. Le Bas C.W., 'Life of T.F. Middleton' (London 1831).

40. Lincoln's Inn — information from Lincoln's Inn Librarian.

41. Markham J., 'Parliamentary elections in East Yorkshire' (East Yorkshire Local History Society 1982).

42. Menzies-Wilson J. & Lloyd H., 'Amelia: the tale of a Plain Friend' (O.U.P. 1937).

43. Methodist Conference — Minutes of 1829 Conference.

44. 'Methodist Magazine', 1837, pages 885-899.

45. Midhurst — 'A history of the representation of Sussex from the earliest period to 1831' (Pub. R. Lee 1832).

46. Moorehead A., 'Darwin & the Beagle' (Hamish Hamilton 1969).

47. More H., 'Coelebs in search of a wife' (1808).

48. Moyse-Bartlett H., 'The pirates of Trucial Oman' (Macdonald 1966).

49. Neave D., & Waterson E., 'Lost houses of East Yorkshire' (East Yorkshire Local History Society 1988).

50. Oliver G., 'The history and antiquities of Beverley' (Beverley 1829).

51. Oman C., 'Nelson' (Hodder & Stoughton 1947).

52. Opie A., 'Lays for the dead' (London 1834).

53. Philips C.H., 'The East India Company 1784-1836' (Manchester University Press 1961).

54. Pollock J., 'Wilberforce' (Constable 1977).

55. Poulson G., 'Beverlac: the antiquities & history of Beverley' (London 1829).

56. Poulson G., 'History & antiquities of the Seigniory of Holderness' (Hull & London 1838).

57. Queens' College Cambridge — information from Queens' College Librarian.

58. Renier G.J., 'The ill-fated princess: the life of Charlotte, daughter of the Prince Regent' (Peter Davies 1932).

59. Semmel B., 'The Methodist revolution' (Heinemann 1974).

59a. Sheahan J.J., 'History & description of Kingston upon Hull' (London 1864).

60. Sheppard T., 'The evolution of Kingston upon Hull' (A. Brown & Sons, Hull 1911).

61. Shoreham parish registers — entries in family papers.

62. Simpson H., 'The history of the Hull Royal Infirmary' (1888).

63. Smiths & Thompson's bank — extracts from ledgers in National Westminster Bank archives, London, with information from the Archivist.
64. Southey R., 'The life of Wesley, and the rise & progress of Methodism' (1820).
65. St George's Hospital, London — information from Hospital Archivist.
66. Swine parish registers, in Humberside County Record Office.
67. Thomis M., 'The Luddites' (David & Charles 1970).
68. *Thompson C.W., — letters from Malta & Egypt, 1810-1811, in Cambridge University Library, ref. MS Oo.vi.96 No. 20.
69. *Thompson E., — Chapter 17 of draft biography of Thomas Perronet Thompson in Brynmor Jones Library, Hull University, ref. DTH/5.
70. *Thompson E.V., 'En Quenouille: a record of the family Perronet-Thompson (1969, unpublished).
71. Thompson P.P., [Mrs Thompson] — letter to her son Thomas in Brotherton Library, Leeds, ref. RHD.FMZ.vi.71.
71a. Thompson P.P., 'Observations in Scotland in the summer of 1807' (journal). Property of *Mr Nigel Hughes.
72. Thompson T., [Thomas Thompson] — letter in 'English Historical Documents' Vol. xi. p.664.
73. Thompson T., [ibid], 'Ocellum Promontorium: or short observations on the ancient state of Holderness' (Hull 1821).
74. Thompson T., [ibid], 'Historic facts relating to the sea port & market town of Ravenspurne' (Hull 1822).
75. Thompson T., [ibid], 'The history of the church & priory of Swine' (Hull 1824).
76. Thompson T., [ibid] — last will & testament, 1824 (copy owned by the author).
77. *Thompson T.P., — catalogue of exhibition at Brotherton Library, Leeds, 1971.
78. *Thompson T. P., — letter to the Adjutant, Grenadier Guards, 1866, in Brynmor Jones Library, Hull University.
78a. *Thompson T.P., letter to his father, 1823, in Brotherton Library, Leeds, ref. RHD/FMZ/vi.71.
79. Thorne R.G. (ed), 'The House of Commons 1790-1816' Vol. V (Secker & Warburg 1986).
80. Townsend W.J., Workman H.B., & Ayrs G., 'A new history of Methodism', Vol. I (Hodder & Stoughton 1909).
81. Turner H.A.B., 'A collector's guide to Staffordshire pottery figures' (MacGibbon & Kee 1971).
82. Tyerman L., 'The life & times of the Rev John Wesley' (Hodder & Stoughton 1870).
82a. Venn J. & J.A., 'Alumni Cantabrigiensis' (C.U.P. 1922).
83. Victoria History of the East Riding, Vol. 6 (OUP 1989).
84. Villiers A., 'Captain Cook: the seamen's seaman' (Hodder & Stoughton 1967).
85. Waite V., 'The Bristol Hotwell' (Bristol, c.1980).
86. Waterson E., 'Cottingham Castle' (Georgian Society for East Yorkshire, Issue 13, 1986).
87. 'West Briton', 14th February 1823.
88. Wells R.A.E., 'Dearth & distress in Yorkshire 1793-1802' (Borthwick Papers No. 52, 1977).
89. Wesley, Charles — Journal Vol. 2.
90. Wesley, John — Journal.
91. Wesley, John — Letters.
92. Whitaker T.D., 'History of Richmondshire' (1823) — table of Wycliffe family of Gailes.
93. Whitby Museum — information from Hon. Keeper.
94. Wilberforce R.I. & S., 'The life of William Wilberforce' (John Murray 1838).
95. Wilberforce W., — letter to C.W. Thompson, with reply (1812) — in Brynmor Jones Library, Hull, ref. DTH.1.4.61.
96. Wilberforce W., — letter (1797) to Arthur Young, in British Museum, ref. Add. MSS 35127 f.449.

Index